Solving *Math* Problems Kids Care About

Randall J. Souviney
University of California, San Diego

Good Year Books
Tucson, Arizona

Dedication

For my grandchildren—Torin, Shannon, Bjorn and Rhiannon . . .
I hope this book helps you figure things out.

Good Year Books are available for most basic curriculum subjects plus many enrichment areas. For more Good Year Books, contact your local bookseller or educational dealer. For a complete catalog with information about other Good Year Books, please contact:

Good Year Books
P.O. Box 91858
Tucson, AZ 85752-1858
www.goodyearbooks.com

Illustrations: David Fischer & Karen Tafoya
Design: Performance Design

ISBN-10: 1-59647-061-5
ISBN-13: 978-1-59647-061-3
Previous ISBN: 0-673-16534-5
1 2 3 4 5 6 7 8 9 -VH- 12 11 10 09 08 07 06 05

Library of Congress Cataloging-in-Publication Data

Souviney, Randall J.
 Solving math problems kids care about /
  Randall J. Souviney, —2nd ed.
 Rev. ed. of: Solving problems kids care about. c1981
 Includes biographical references.
 ISBN 1-59647-061-5 (alk. paper)
 1. Problem solving—Study and teaching.
 2. Mathematics—Study and teaching. 3. Activity programs in education. I. Souviney, Randall J. Solving problems kids care about. II. Title

QA63.S65.2005
372.7—dc22
                                         2005050804

CONTENTS

Section III: Reproducible Problem Starters 96

Introduction

This little book has had much longer legs than I could have possibly anticipated when I finished the manuscript twenty-five years ago in the highlands of Papua New Guinea. When the publisher asked me to update the book, I wanted to do more than give it a fresh look. I felt it important to maintain the integrity of the original approach to teaching problem solving that has been used successfully in so many classrooms over the past two decades. I was grateful for the opportunity to clarify the description of problem-solving strategies and classroom pedagogy and to include some new problems to challenge and, hopefully, amuse. I also gratefully corrected a few errors in the original text pointed out to me over the years by a few persistent students who learned not to believe everything they read in books.

The world has changed considerably since Ronald Reagan was president—the Berlin Wall has come down and the countries to the east have joined with Europe, humanity somehow managed to transition to the twenty-first century without great event (a year early, but that is another story), 911 took on new meaning in the world, and the ubiquitous cell phone has become far more powerful than the computer I used to write the original manuscript for this book. However, a clear-thinking citizenry has never been more important than now as we learn to face the uncertainty of the post-Cold-War era. High-quality mathematics education offers one of the best opportunities for our children to learn problem-solving skills to help them make thoughtful, evidence-based judgments so important to good citizenship, and, just maybe, foster harmony among the peoples of the world.

Over the past twenty-five years, mathematics textbooks have become increasingly narrow in both content and pedagogy. School leaders have reacted to the poor performance of our children on international tests by significantly increasing the emphasis on routine calculations. Problem solving, when it appears at all, is embedded in lessons largely populated with worked examples and routine exercises. This national trend toward the adoption of curriculum that focuses on the development of algorithms had led to improved test scores on arithmetic and algebraic operations. However, student performance on mathematical applications and problem solving continues to be frustratingly weak among all the socioeconomic levels, but particularly among children from low-income families.

Readers familiar with the original text will find, in this second edition, increased attention to story problems, an expanded description of problem-solving strategies, inclusive strategies for students with special needs, ideas about embedded assessment, and ten new problems. I hope both those of you who are new and those who are returning readers will find these pages a worthy supplement to your mathematics instruction and will help you provide students with engaging practice with problem-solving strategies and improve their mathematical thinking.

This book would not have been possible without drawing upon the respected work of other mathematics teachers, most notably Marilyn Burns, Martin Gardner, Carol Greenes, George Polya, and Dale Seymour. Several people helped with the development of the manuscript for the first edition of this book, including Kiri Mimi, who created the original illustrations at the same time he was working on the first mathematics textbooks published in Papua New Guinea; Gail Anders, Lauyang Posanau, and Priscilla Warbat who prepared the initial manuscript; and Joan Akers and John Wavrik, who generously offered many suggestions to improve the problem descriptions and solutions. I want to thank Andrea Cheng and Sarah Moulton for assisting with the preparation of the manuscript and Bobbie Dempsey for her editorial guidance on the second edition, and especially Stephanie for her curiously improved navigation skills and loving care as we explored South America searching for these pages.

R.J.S.
Buenos Aires
January 2005

How to Use This Book

You do not need to be an expert problem solver to teach effective problem-solving skills, but it sure helps! Our primary role as teachers is to establish a nonthreatening environment to encourage efficient problem-solving behaviors among our students. We must also have the courage to learn along with our students, because many of these important problem-solving skills may be as new to us as to our classes. Here are a few hints that you may find helpful:

1. Scan through section I (especially chapter 2) to review strategies and techniques for teaching mathematical problem solving. In particular, look at:
   a. Problems Worth Solving
   b. A Four-step Problem-solving Plan, including the strategies listed in step 2 of the plan.
2. Think about how to organize your classroom to foster effective problem-solving sessions. The following sequence is suggested:
   a. Begin with the whole-class problem-solving warm-up activities to encourage divergent thinking and cooperative problem-solving behavior.
   b. Discuss each particular strategy in a large group (for example, *working backward*). Break up into groups of four and assign everyone the same problem (perhaps "Stack the Deck").
   c. Introduce each strategy in this way, allowing ample time for a whole-class discussion after each session to encourage a sharing of strategies and solutions.
   d. As you and your students become more adept at using various solution strategies, offer a choice of problems. Always allow time for discussion.

3. Other recommendations:
   a. Initial problem-solving sessions should be brief. Extend the duration with experience.
   b. Try to schedule sessions frequently, at least twice a week.
   c. Initially, plan a whole-class discussion after each session. Later, these large-group discussions may be required less frequently.
   d. Every child (group) may be unable to completely solve every problem in the time available. The problems are designed, however, so that everyone is encouraged to make some progress and offer input during the discussions.
   e. The Problem-Starter sheets should be reproduced for each child. The hints provided should help individuals (or groups) formulate a solution strategy.
   f. The problems are sequenced so that they become increasingly complex. With sufficient experience, intermediate and junior-high level students should be successful in solving most of the problems, while the more complex examples may be inappropriate for younger children.
   g. After working through the problems of interest in this book, perhaps you and your class might enjoy enlargeing your collection by reviewing the sources in the bibliography or asking people in your community. Keep in mind the section criteria in chapter 1 when choosing your "problems worth solving."

Section I

Mathematical Problem Solving

Chapter 1
What's Worth Knowing

As our world changes before our eyes—our knowledge base becoming obsolete at an alarming rate and value systems seeming to change with or without us—what do we teach our children who must survive and prosper in a changing environment we may scarcely be able to imagine? What is worth teaching today that will be worth knowing in twenty years?

In virtually every field, accepted practices are becoming obsolete as rapidly as new knowledge develops. Teachers find it more and more difficult to remain current in their profession as the years pass. Teachers must search for the essential strands that transcend the blizzard of competing ideologies and techniques in order to function effectively in their classrooms. Specialization, the traditional mechanism designed to contend with information explosion, will continue to play a significant role in our lives. The time is long past when one individual has possessed a thorough understanding of an entire field. (Karl Gauss is purported to be the last individual to understand all contemporary mathematics, and he died more than a hundred years ago. We have developed more mathematics in the past twenty years than in the thousands of years before Gauss!)

Clearly, we must look at learning differently if the children in our schools today are to gain a sense of competence in their lives. Facts and relationships between facts will become less important, learned temporarily and later replaced by a new set of relevant facts and relationships. We are discovering that many of the "facts" associated with everyday life are reflections of our own values and may not be valid in other societies. Ethnocentric thinking, though comfortable, will be less useful in a shrinking, diverse world.

A good knowledge of mathematics is increasingly important, although some skills are proving more valuable than others. Manual computation will continue to play an important role, though we now depend more and more on the speed and accuracy of calculators for large computations. There is little value to methodically deriving the wrong answer to ten decimal places. The ability to understand and solve naturally occurring problems is increasingly a prized attribute. Facts are important to the extent that they enable the understanding of a particular problem. Robust solution strategies remain useful for solving a range of related problems.

PROBLEMS WORTH SOLVING

Before turning our attention to specific problem-solving teaching strategies, we will first discuss the characteristics of problem situations appropriate for novice problem solvers. Here, novice refers to level of problem-solving experience, rather than one's age. An ideal problem situation should:

1. be readily understandable to the student, yet the solution should not be immediately apparent.
2. be intrinsically motivating and intellectually stimulating.
3. have more than one solution path.
4. require only previously learned arithmetic operations and concepts.
5. lend itself to being solved over a reasonable period of time (not a simple computational procedure).
6. be somewhat open-ended (solutions should suggest new problems).
7. integrate various subject areas—mathematics, science, social studies, and fine arts.
8. be defined well enough so you will know when it's solved.

Convergent and Divergent Problems

These eight criteria do not characterize the type of problems found in most textbooks. Word problems typically ask students to decide which operation(s) to apply to the values provided. Though many problems encountered in life involve quantities (counting, measures, money), rarely are these values presented in an organized, symbolic form. An individual first must recognize that a problem exists and be motivated to seek understanding. This initial, seemingly aimless, trial-and-error stage

of problem solving generally includes doodling, sketching, estimating, measuring, counting, asking questions, and listening. With children it is especially important to encourage the exploration of ideas and concrete models to define problem parameters and eventual solution strategies. Most of all, such problems offer children a glimpse of the creative act that teachers, engineers, accountants, mothers, politicians, architects, and scientists are engaged in daily—namely, the deconstruction of complex events (analysis) and organizing familiar elements (synthesis) to derive order and meaning from novel problem situations.

The following example illustrates the type of problem situation that is easy to describe yet requires quite a bit of "messing about" with ideas and sketches to fully define the problem situation and predict an appropriate solution strategy.

Billiard Table Math

Suppose you have a rectangular billiard table like the one below. If you shoot out from the lower left corner at 45° (split the corner square), which corner will the ball end up in?

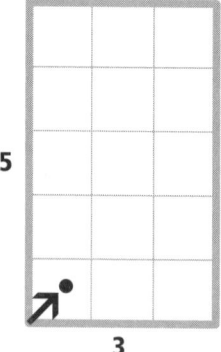

Figure 1.1

First, it is not at all clear that the ball will end up in any corner. Also, you have to realize that a billiard ball bounces off at the same angle it strikes the cushion (45°, in this case). It might require a bit of experimenting to justify this one element of the problem. One convenient way to test your skill is to sketch the table on 1-cm graph paper and trace the path of the ball.

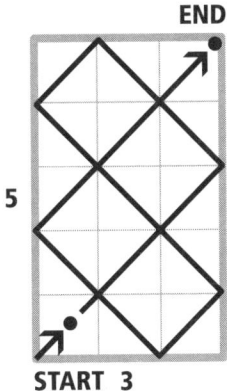

Figure 1.2

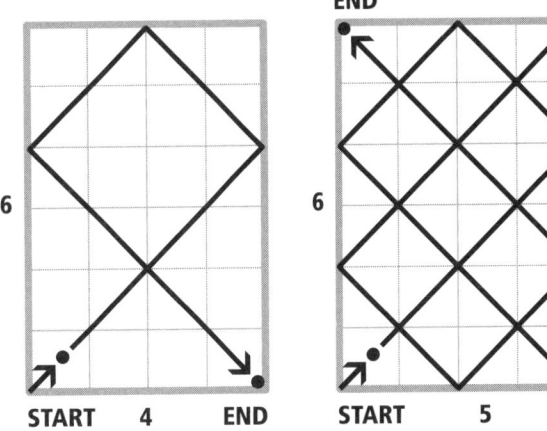

This odd-sized table (conventional size is 3 x 6) provides an "interesting" game, finishing in the upper right corner. Notice that the ball crosses every square. Is this true for other-sized rectangular tables? Will the ball always end in a corner (assume the dimensions are whole units)? Can you predict which corner the ball will end in, without tracing its path? (To keep things simple, remember to shoot out from the lower left corner at 45°.)

Each of these questions is easy to understand, but the solution is not immediately apparent. The solution to the initial problem raises several new and interesting questions. The intellectual and motor skills necessary to effectively participate in this problem should be available to most students age nine or older. The situation is motivating and intellectually stimulating to most children. It's reasonably easy to determine when you have solved the problem. Based on our problem selection criteria, this problem seems to be an ideal candidate for classroom use.

Let's continue our game. One strategy is to try out tables of various sizes and see if any useful insight is gained from the results or if a pattern emerges. This state of experimentation not only allows the collection of potentially useful data, but also encourages a high level of involvement on the part of the solver. As we will discuss later, motivation and mind-set play a significant role in effective problem solving.

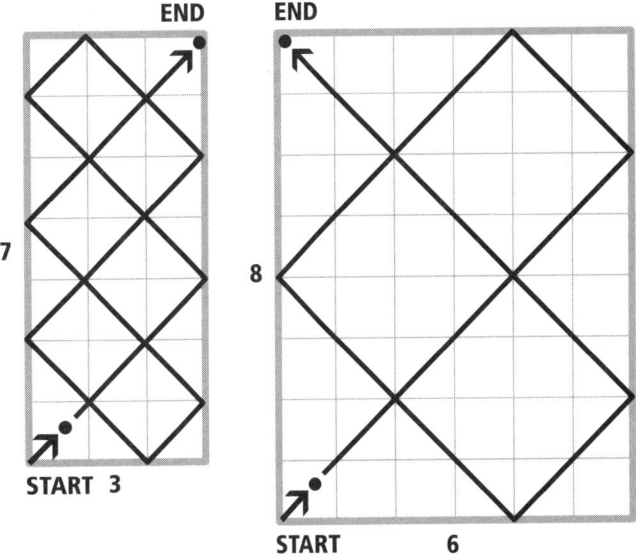

Figure 1.3

"Interesting" or "Boring" Game

Do table dimensions determine if a game is interesting (every square crossed by the ball) or boring (some squares not crossed)? Perhaps a table would help organize the data we collected. Using graph paper, play the billiard games listed in Table 1.1 on page 8 and verify that each table is "interesting" or "boring." Play a few additional games and enter those data as well. The first number of each pair represents the length of the base of the table (horizontal axis) and the second number represents the height (vertical axis).

Table 1.1

Billiard Games

INTERESTING	BORING
(3,5)	(4,6)
(5,6)	(6,8)
(3,7)	(4,10)
(4,9)	(3,9)
(5,4)	(4,4)
(,)	(,)

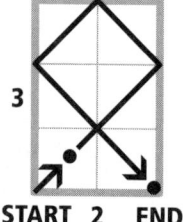

3

START 2 END

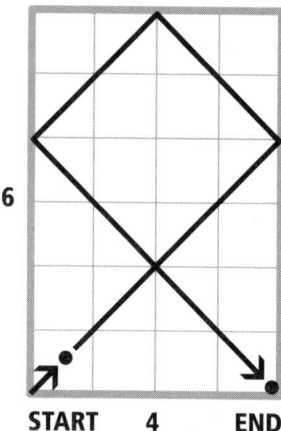

6

START   4   END

Looking at the number pairs, put your pattern recognition skills to work. How are the number pairs for the interesting games alike? How are they different from *all* the boring games? At this point in the solution process, past experience in looking for number patterns and recent experience in generating examples of billiard games must somehow foster the critical moment of inspiration. There are no guarantees in creative problem solving. If the light doesn't shine, one has three choices:

1. Continue generating data using the present strategy, hoping some key element is just around the corner.
2. Try a new strategy.
3. Let the problem "rest" a few days and then try again.

The inspiration in this case involves observing the relationship between the first and second number in each pair. Notice that for an interesting game, the number pairs have no factors (other than 1) in common (e.g., [3, 7], [3, 5], [5, 6]). This is not the case for boring games (e.g., [4, 6], [4, 10], [6, 8]). Another way of looking at, or "modeling," the situation is to consider each pair a fraction, or ratio. Interesting games can't be reduced (e.g., 3/7, 3/5, 5/6), while boring games can be (e.g., 4/6, 4/10, 6/8).

A "family" of billiard tables can be constructed, opening a whole new area of investigation. In Figure 1.4, notice the similar pattern the ball makes for each game in the (2, 3) family (the smallest table at the top). Is this true for other tables in the family [e.g., (3, 4), (6, 8), (9, 12)]? Will the ball end up in the same corner for every game in a family? Will this

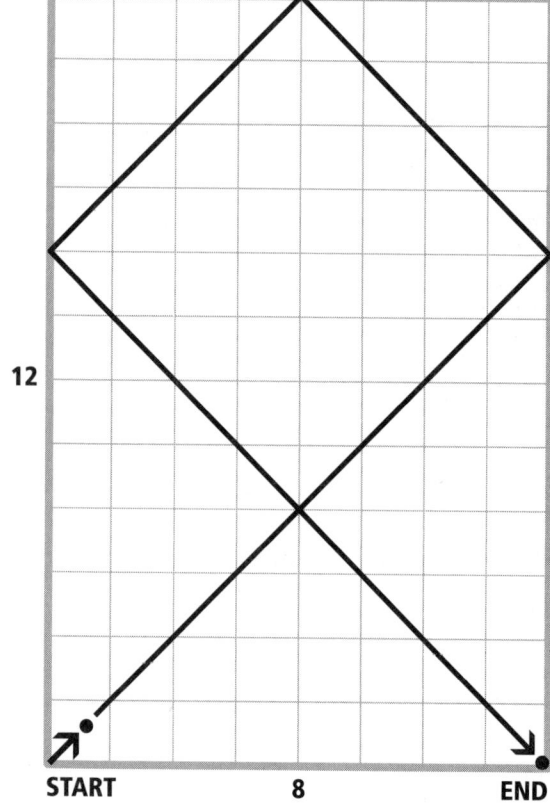

12

START   8   END

Figure 1.4

information help us predict which corner ball will end up in for all games?

Completing Table 1.2 by collecting data on *interesting* games only should make the situation more transparent. If you systematically worked out all the examples in the table, you may have discovered that every boring game has an interesting family member that ends in the same corner.

Table 1.2
The Ball Stops Here

LOWER LEFT	UPPER LEFT	UPPER RIGHT	LOWER RIGHT
	(3,4)	(3,7)	(4,5)
	(5,6)	(5,9)	(6,7)
	(7,8)	(5,7)	(4,9)
	(,)	(,)	(,)

Again, recognizing a pattern that distinguishes among the columns should inspire an "aha" experience. A simple way to describe the solution is that, for an interesting game, the ball always stops at the end of the even axis. If there is no even axis (e.g., [5, 7]), the ball ends in the upper right-hand corner (i.e., it never returns to its starting point).

The last step in the process is to convince yourself that your solution is true for all cases. Generally, it is not necessary to construct a formal proof at this level. Unless it is a life-and-death situation or you're risking the family fortune, working out a few well-chosen examples should suffice. This "proof by desire" should be held tentatively, ready to be altered as necessary to accommodate any conflicting data that might arise in subsequent experiments.

A Word about "Real-world" Problems

Problems found in math books (including this one) generally differ from real-world problems in two important ways, and the success you and your students enjoy when applying the techniques discussed here and in the next chapter to practical problems encountered in daily life will depend greatly on your ability to understand and compensate for these distinctions.

First, some problems in everyday life may have no solution under the naturally occurring conditions.

Remember those carefully stated conditions found in most "school" problems: You can remove one marble at a time, return it to the bag and shake. The implicit conditions are also relatively transparent: Don't look up the answer in the back of the book! With real-world problems the conditions, both stated and implicit, become far more important.

For example, consider the ongoing world oil crisis. Prior to 1970, most people realized that petroleum supplies were limited and were rapidly being depleted by an energy-hungry world. The problem for the United States became one of meeting the growing energy demand of industry and the public. Several solutions were suggested, including conservation, increasing automobile mileage, finding new domestic oil fields, manufacturing synthetic fuels, instituting higher import quotas, or introducing alternative energy sources.

The most frequently used solution has been to increase import quotas. The problem today remains the same, but the conditions have now changed. The complex Middle East situation has made the sales of crude oil far more than an economic decision. New atomic power plants remain politically unacceptable, yet many people still cannot afford to heat their homes during the winter.

Each generation discovers that real-world problems are almost never permanently solved. When trouble arises, new solutions must be found to meet new conditions. Strategies originally considered and discarded may suddenly show new promise. For example, solar panels and windmills have become more competitive as sources of electricity, not only due to improvements in technology but also because oil and gas have significantly increased cost.

The second distinction between "textbook" and "real-world" problems is related to the underlying values and beliefs of the solver. If the solution to a problem is persistently elusive, it is always wise to check your assumptions. Values conflicts occur when two individuals experience the same event and arrive at two opposing points of view and, based on their own value systems, each is absolutely correct. When this occurs, a solution to the conflict may be impossible unless one or both sets of values are compromised. Values conflicts occur between age groups, political parties, and socioeconomic groups, and, especially, in culturally diverse environments.

These practical social problems, which show up in classrooms, at customer relations desks at department stores, and in the international political arena, are often exasperatingly difficult to solve. One common pitfall is failing to recognize that a values conflict is at the heart of the problem in the first place—the solver assumes everyone involved in the situation has a common understanding of the events. Solutions to real-world problems often require a deep understanding of each other's value system, considerable mutual respect, and an overall balance of power. Violating these conditions often invites an argument in the classroom—or a real war if sufficient national interest is at stake.

The techniques described in this book are useful in solving a limited class of nonroutine problems. In the real world, such methods certainly contribute to the solution of practical problems but may not be sufficient in themselves to unravel the complex problems societies create.

TWO TYPES OF REASONING

Regressive and progressive reasoning are two characteristic approaches to solving novel problems. Both were originally described by the Greeks and have been subsequently refined by mathematicians and scientists over the past 2,000 years. Figure 1.5 shows how regressive and progressive reasoning have complementary features that, when applied appropriately, can assist in planning and implementing a solution strategy.

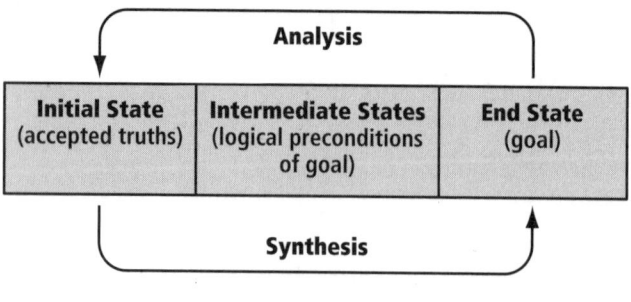

Figure 1.5

Analysis (regressive reasoning) is the process of logically working through a problem backward. Beginning with a well-defined (though not completely understood) problem description, the solver searches for a simpler condition that, if true, will guarantee the solution of the original problem.

Analysis continually reduces the complexity of a situation until the interrelationships between all the preconditions of the problem become clear.

For example, if you found yourself stranded miles from the nearest gas station because a prankster let the air out of your bicycle tire, a simple precondition that guarantees you will be back on the road is to somehow refill your tire. By continuing the process of deducing appropriate preconditions, you eventually arrive at a condition that can be easily satisfied—perhaps temporarily filling the tire with water. Your analysis should lead directly to a plan that can then be carried out by repeating the steps in the opposite direction (simplest to most complex). This complementary process is called *synthesis* (progressive reasoning). Any error in logic made during the analytical phase will be revealed graphically during the implementation of the solution plan—it may take all night to fill the tire with water!

Most problems require the coordinated application of both processes, though as problems become more routine, less analysis may be needed.

Ends-Means Analysis

An alternative way of thinking about these reciprocal methods of reasoning is a process called *ends-means analysis*. *Ends* refers to a clear statement of the goal or intent. The better the "end" is described for a given problem, the easier the solution. The means consist of a set of known concepts and principles that can be brought to bear on the given situation.

The first step when applying ends-means analysis is to state your goal clearly so you will know when you have solved the problem. In many cases, this initial step requires a good deal of thought and experimentation. The results of your efforts, however, will be well worth the trouble.

Once a clear goal has been established, the next step is to determine a sequence of actions that, if carried out, will ensure a satisfactory solution (analysis). Finally, as each step in the solution process is carried out (synthesis), the current state of the situation is examined and compared to the desired result. If the degree of misfit has diminished, the plan is continued. If not, the problem and solution plan are reexamined. Ends-means analysis embodies the analysis of the problem situation, the development of a sequence of actions, and a scheme for monitoring the syntheses of these actions as you work toward a solution.

Structured Problem Solving

Computer science provides another view the problem-solving process. The first step in structured problem solving is to establish a well-defined goal. Using analysis, a "tree" of independent subgoals is determined that are preconditions for the desired result. This "chunking" process is continued with each subgoal until all the individual tasks are well known (primitive). Finally, through synthesis, the process is reversed; individual subgoals are accomplished and coordinated with each other. If the process is successful, the original need will be satisfied. If not, the goal must be reviewed in light of the error and the analysis resumed anew.

As the low-level chunks and their uses become more familiar to the user, less analysis may be required. When a set of related chunks becomes completely generalized, a whole class of problems can be addressed by relying on a synthesis of these well-known chunks. For example, in attempting to design a ship's hull that will be very stable in rough seas, a novice might have to build several models before

discovering the optimum combination of length, width, depth, and shape (analysis). An experienced builder draws upon a well-coordinated set of skills (chunks) that allow him to confidently predict hull performance characteristics (synthesis).

The sample tree diagram in Figure 1.6 provides a practical example of planning a backpacking trip. Many implicit conditions apply to the problem of going backpacking. Each situation is unique. The solution below is but one example of the key considerations that may be taken into account when planning a trip. The primitive chunks (lowest-level tasks on each branch) must be coordinated in order to synthesize a solution. For example, if money isn't obtained prior to going to the store, embarrassment may ensue. It is possible to make the solution more elegant (efficient) if, for example, all the trips to the store are combined in one journey. It is interesting to note that the set of primitive (known) chunks that solve a particular problem may not be unique. Their order as well as their content may vary.

Regardless of what convenient structure we use to explain creative problem solving, an intangible element remains that defies rigorous description yet seems fundamental to the entire enterprise. Factual knowledge and past problem-solving experience

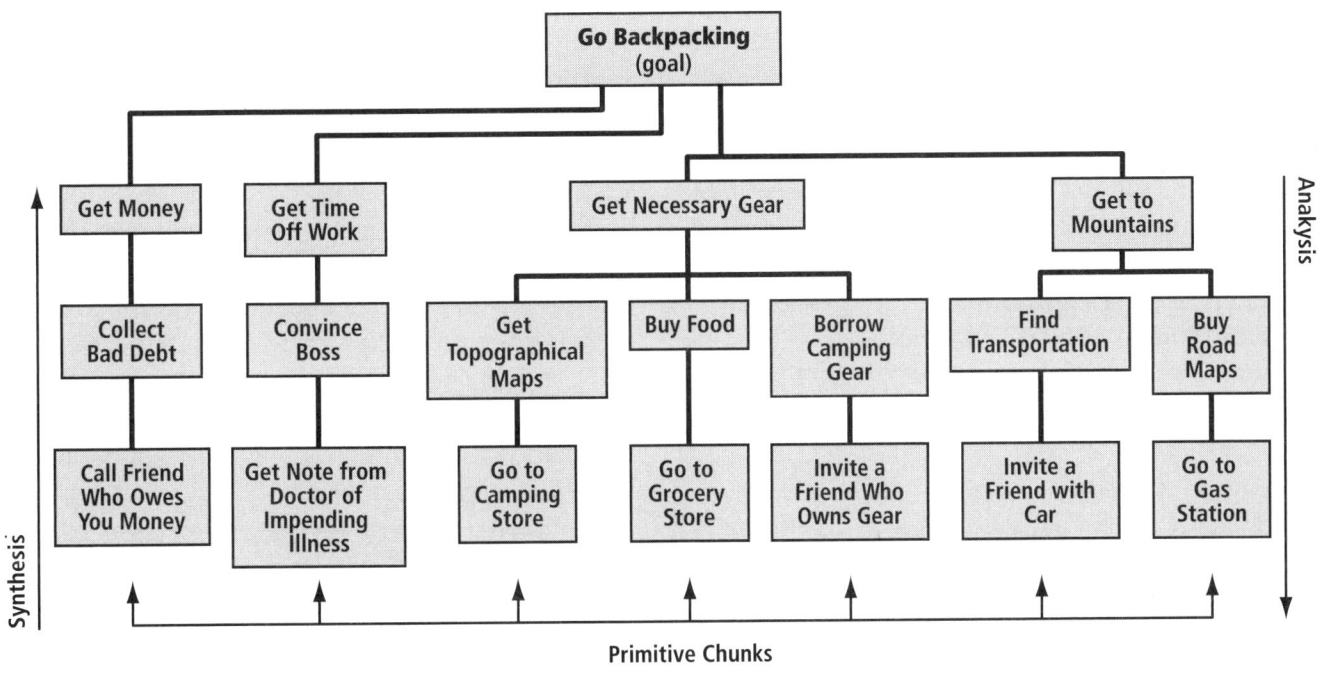

Structured Problem-solving Tree

Figure 1.6

are certainly important; however, an element of chance pervades any novel problem situation. An effective problem solver must not only possess appropriate skills and knowledge to bring to bear on the situation, but he or she must also have the motivation, persistence, and self-confidence to risk failure in pursuing a satisfactory solution. Though "chance favors the prepared mind," it takes courage to see a truly novel problem through to a satisfactory solution.

Chapter 2 introduces a four-step problem-solving plan, originally proposed by George Polya. This plan will help students organize their use of analysis and synthesis to solve problems.

SUMMARY

Learning effective strategies and skills for solving novel problems is becoming more important in our rapidly changing world. Schools must prepare students for a world that is certain to be far more complex and challenging than today. To develop such problem-solving skills, teachers must carefully choose problem situations that offer a balance of divergent and convergent elements. A problem worth solving:

1. should be understandable, yet the solution should not be readily apparent.
2. should be motivating and easy to describe.
3. has more than one solution path.
4. requires skills and concepts appropriate for the grade level.
5. should be solvable over a reasonable time period.
6. is open-ended whereby solutions suggest new questions to be investigated.
7. should integrate several subject areas (science, social studies, fine arts, mathematics).
8. should be well defined so you will know when it's solved.

The more a particular problem exhibits these criteria, the greater potential it has for developing healthy problem-solving attitudes and skills in children and all novice problem solvers. In general, a good problem should require a high level of involvement on the part of the solver—making models or sketches, doing experiments, collecting and organizing data, and searching for patterns and generalizations. Such interaction enhances the child's understanding of the problem situation, generates clues that weren't evident in the problem description, and aids the selection of an appropriate solution strategy.

Real-world problems differ from typical mathematics problems in two important ways. The solution of everyday problems depends far more on explicit and implicit *conditions* than do the well-defined examples found in problem books. In fact, many real-world problems may have no solution at all under the existing conditions. The second distinction involves the human factor of *values conflicts*. Many of the most difficult problems in society resist solution because of these underlying differences in worldview. The strategies described in this book may be useful in addressing such problem situations but are not sufficient in themselves to unravel the complexities of human interaction.

Mathematical problem solving depends on two basic types of reasoning:

1. Analysis, or regressive reasoning
2. Synthesis, or progressive reasoning

Knowledge of these two processes is fundamental to understanding general problem-solving plans such as ends-means analysis and structured problem solving. Ends-means analysis and structured problem solving both involve the analysis of a problem situation as a set of well-defined actions and the synthesis of these actions as you work toward a solution.

Ends-means analysis refers to a process of carefully describing a desired result (end) and determining a sequence of actions (means) that seem to ensure a satisfactory solution. Subsequently, when carrying out each step in the solution process, the current status is compared to the desired result in order to monitor progress and make appropriate adjustments in the solution.

Structured problem solving is a process of constructing a "tree" of independent subgoals (chunks) that together form a complete set of preconditions for the desired result. These subgoals are further subdivided until they reach a "primitive" or known state. Reversing the process completes the solution.

Chapter 2
Teaching Mathematical Problem Solving

Children are naturally wired with the desire to understand their world. Learning to use mathematical ideas can empower children to be more systematic in their explorations and more accurate in their predictions about how things work. The following story illustrates different ways a problem might be addressed by three people with various problem-solving backgrounds.

An engineer, a mathematician, and an anthropologist were taking wilderness training and their instructor was giving a session on desert survival. He said that a person stranded in the desert—alone, without water, but within sight of an oasis—should walk half the distance to the oasis, then rest, then walk half the remaining distance, rest again, and continue this procedure until reaching the oasis.

- The mathematician immediately observed that this procedure would always result in dying of thirst. She claimed that if, after each rest, the thirsty traveler walked only half the remaining distance to the oasis, there would be an infinite number of rest stops and therefore the person would never quite arrive! Her solution was to walk halfway plus one step after each rest.
- The engineer agreed with the mathematician's logic but recognized that real-world problems often do not exactly follow their underlying mathematical models. In this case, he was sure that he could get close enough to the oasis using the recommended procedure to eventually lean over and drink from the oasis well.
- The anthropologist thought that it would take more time to walk to the oasis than was possible during daylight hours and questioned whether it would be possible to estimate half the distance

to the oasis at night. Observing that animals and people who live in the desert generally travel in the cool of the night, he pointed out that by following the local custom the traveler should rest during the day and walk as far as possible during the night, using the stars to guide the way.

Each of these solutions appears logical once you understand the underlying assumptions of each solver. Mathematical models can often motivate critical insights necessary to solve theoretical problems. To determine if the solution is realistic, however, one needs to validate the result by conducting an experiment. Finally, an experimental solution should be evaluated against competing solutions to determine if it is socially acceptable.

Even simple counting games can lead to unexpected insights when the moves are explored systematically. For example, let's explore the game of multi-pile NIM. In this game, fifteen counters are positioned in three rows of seven, five, and three counters.

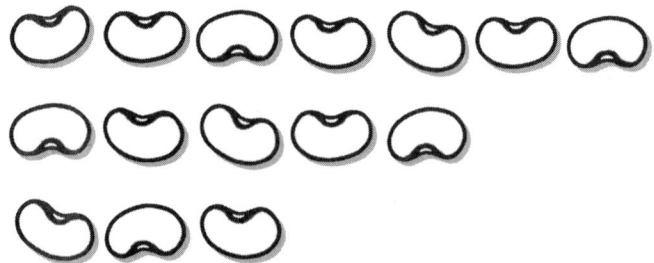

Multi-pile NIM Game
Figure 2.1

Rules: Two players take turns removing one or more counters from any one row. Each player may remove counters from only one row on each turn but may switch to another row on the next turn. The player removing the last of the counters wins.

Players improve their NIM playing skill as they learn to recognize winning patterns. For example, one of the first patterns players generally discover is that if they can leave their opponent faced with two equal rows, they can always win. For example, regardless of how many counters Caleb removes from either of the two equal rows, Kaitlyn can make the rows equal again by removing the same number of counters from the other row. Eventually, Kaitlyn will be left with the last counter to remove (see Figure

2.2). By working backward from states of parity (demonstrated by the paired rows in the example), it is possible to establish a series of moves that guarantees the first player will win regardless of how Caleb moves.

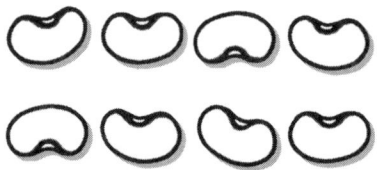

Winning Strategy,
Figure 2.2

The technique of leaving two equal rows forces your opponent to break the *parity*, which allows Kaitlyn to restore the parity and eventually prevail. However, understanding a far more powerful form of mathematical parity enables an expert player to win a game of NIM containing any number of rows with any number of counters in each. This involves mentally grouping the counters in each row by powers-of-2. Begin by making the largest groups possible in each row, starting with 4 counters, then 2s, then 1s. For three-row NIM, the starting display is out of parity because the rows contain three 1s, two 2s, and two 4s.

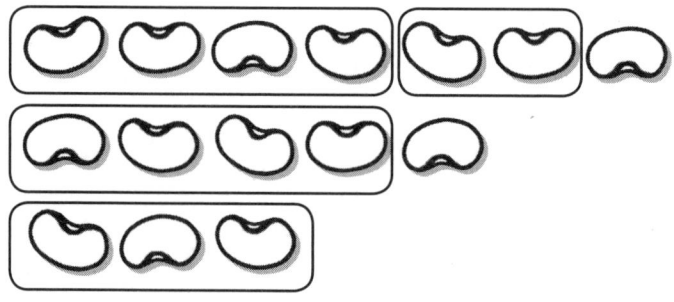

Base 2 Parity
Figure 2.3

If Kaitlyn removes one counter from any row at the start of the game, it leaves Caleb with pairs of 1s, 2s, and 4s. No matter how many counters Caleb removes from any one row, the parity between the base-2 groupings will be broken. Kaitlyn can then restore base-2 parity by removing equivalent counters from another row. Eventually, Kaitlyn will be left with a single row and will win the game.

This strategy can be applied to other NIM games. To play four-row NIM, add one more counter as a fourth row. Notice that by adding a fourth row containing one 1 counter, the starting arrangement already has base-2 parity (four 1s, two 2s, and two 4s). Therefore, the second player, Caleb, has the advantage in this game. No matter what counters Kaitlyn removes, Caleb can create a state of base-2 parity, therefore forcing Kaitlyn to break the parity. Eventually, Caleb will prevail if he follows the base-2 parity strategy systematically. Play several different starting arrangements of NIM and see how the base-2 parity strategy can be used to give you the winning advantage. This powerful base-2 parity strategy offers a generalized, or deterministic, plan for winning many different types of counting games.

CHARACTERISTICS OF GOOD PROBLEM SOLVERS

Cognitive research indicates that students who are successful at solving problems tend to focus on the problem's underlying mathematical structure. Novice problem solvers often attend to irrelevant, surface details of the problems, ignoring important structural relationships (Krutetskii, 1976; Silver, 1979).

Good problem solvers also seem to structure mathematical concepts and rules into related chunks that make these solution components easier to recall at appropriate times (Chi, Feltovich & Glaser, 1981). Conversely, novice problem solvers tend to memorize mathematical knowledge as unrelated, discrete rules, making it far more difficult to perceive critical relationships that often play an important role in solving a problem. Such rote learning also makes it more difficult to recognize inconsistencies in a set of procedures (Brown & Burton, 1978).

Good problem solvers also identify pertinent information and ignore irrelevant or superficial problem features, allowing good problem solvers to view a specific problem as but one example of a whole class of similar problems. This critical attribute seems to separate good problem solvers from their less successful peers (Carpenter, 1985).

TYPES OF PROBLEMS

This book introduces students to multiple ways for solving nonroutine problems that involve more than calculation and measurement. To be effective, it is important for teachers to understand the difference between nonroutine process problems and routine calculation story problems found in most elementary textbooks.

Calculation Story Problems

The story problems that appear at the end of textbook chapters are generally designed to provide practice for previously learned concepts and skills. To solve story problems, students read and evaluate the problem statement, evaluate what is known and what is being asked, and finally select the appropriate operation and apply it to the values given (LeBlanc, 1982). As students gain experience, multistep exercises are introduced.

One-step Story Problem

Samantha and Josiah each bought the same stamp for their collection. Samantha paid $14. Josiah paid $1 more. How much did Josiah pay for his stamp?

Multistep Story Problem

Samantha bought two stamps from Josiah, one for $10 and another for $14. Later she sold the first stamp for $12 and the second for $16. How much profit did Samantha make on the sale?

These two examples are typical of routine story problems found in elementary mathematics texts. Notice that all the values included in each problem must be used in the solution. In everyday problem solving, it is generally necessary to select among a range of values present in the problem situation in order to derive a satisfactory solution. In fact, it is often the process of systematically identifying and rejecting extraneous information that makes it difficult to solve real-world problem such as selecting the best mortgage for your family, or picking a stock to hold for retirement.

Other Types of Story Problems

Problems with extraneous or insufficient information are beginning to appear in textbooks; they give students practice in selecting relevant values and identifying missing information required for solution.

Extraneous Information Problem

Samantha bought three stamps from Josiah for $10, $12, and $15. She sold the first two stamps for $14 each. How much profit did Samantha make on the sale?

Missing Information Problem

Samantha bought two stamps from Josiah. She sold the first for $12 and the second for $14. How much profit did Samantha make on the sale?

To introduce such story problems, have students identify the extraneous or missing information in a set of specially prepared story problem cards. It is also advisable to include one or two story problems containing only the required values.

Additional techniques for introducing story problems include:

1. Headline Problems

Write a *headline* summary for a problem. Students supply the story to go with the headline.
Example:

Josiah Has 10 More Stamps Than Samantha
Josiah has 75 stamps. Samantha has 65 stamps. How many more stamps does Josiah have?

2. No-value Problems

Present story problems with *no* specified values. Students are asked to describe (orally or in writing) the solution procedure. Students can supply their own values if they wish.
Example:

Samantha and Josiah each have a large stamp collection. How many stamps do they have altogether?

3. Fill-in Value Problems

Write story problems in which the values must be *filled in* by the students before solving them.
Example:

Josiah has ____ stamps in his collection. He sold ____ stamps to Samantha. How many stamps does Josiah have left?

Nonroutine Process Problems

Process problems differ from story problems in that they cannot be solved immediately after selecting the appropriate operation(s). These problems are generally embedded in more complex contexts then story problems and more effort is initially required to understand the underlying mathematics in order to work toward a solution. Process problems can be used to introduce new skills and concepts or as follow-up activities to apply previously learned mathematical ideas and procedures. Solving process problems requires persistence, flexible thinking, and good organizational skills. Success often relies on one's ability to understand and exploit the underlying mathematical structure of a problem.

The following example offers insight into the different *quality* of mathematical thinking required to solve nonroutine process problems:

Samantha bought a stamp for $10 and sold it to Josiah for $12. Later, she bought it back from Josiah for $14 and resold it to another collector for $16. Did Samantha make a profit on these transactions? If so, how much?

To solve this problem, one must go beyond the misleading surface features implied in the problem statement and question the underlying assumptions. In Samantha's case, at least two seemingly logical explanations might give rise to different amounts of profit:

Explanation 1

Samantha bought the stamp for $10 and sold it to Josiah for $12, giving her a $2 profit. Samantha bought the stamp back from Josiah for $14 at a $2 loss. Finally, Samantha sold the stamp for $16, which gave her a $2 profit. Samantha's total profit was: ($2 − $2) + $2 = $2.

Explanation 2

Samantha bought a stamp for $10 and sold it for $12, giving her a $2 profit. She purchased a stamp for $14 and sold it for $16, giving a $2 profit. Samantha's total profit was: $2 + $2 = $4.

When Samantha reports her profit on her income tax, should the profit for these two transactions be $2 or $4? Only one of the solutions can be correct. Something must be wrong with the assumptions underlying one of these solutions. Explanation 1 assumes that the difference between the first sale ($12) and the repurchase price ($14) counts as a loss. This would be true only if the stamp was never resold. Profit is computed by subtracting the purchase price from the subsequent sale price. Profit on a sale has nothing to do with an object's prior price history. For example, imagine that the price of the stamp jumped to $1,000 after Samantha sold it to Josiah. If Samantha bought it back from Josiah for $1,000 and sold it for $1,002, she would still make a profit of $2 on this transaction plus $2 from the original purchase at $10 and sale of $12, giving a total profit of $4. Based on the solution in Explanation 1, Samantha would have sustained a loss of $1,000 after the second sale of the stamp (i.e., ($2 − $1000) + $2 = −$1000). This extreme example more clearly shows the faulty assumption in Explanation 1.

Explanation 2 correctly assumes no connection between the two transactions because Samantha could have purchased two different stamps, one from Josiah for $10 and another for $14 from someone else. The technique of substituting "extreme" values (like the $1,000 above) into a problem to test the accuracy of your underlying assumptions can be very useful in helping to understand the context of a variety of problems (Ponce & Garrison, 2005).

TEACHING PROBLEM-SOLVING STRATEGIES

Teachers and researchers have identified a set of classroom-tested problem-solving strategies to help students learn to solve process problems (Charles & Lester, 1982; Souviney, 1981; Suydam, 1980). These strategies can be successfully applied to a wide range of problems; alone or in combination, they can help students uncover the mathematical structure underlying novel problem situations. Some strategies may already be familiar and others may be new. Examples of selected strategies are described in "Step 2: Select a Strategy."

Organizing for Problem Solving

Careful planning is required to integrate effectively the use of problem-solving strategies into mathematics instruction. Problem solving rarely involves an uninterrupted line of reasoning from the problem statement to the solution. Students often make false starts and encounter blind alleys. They need to feel comfortable while trying out untested ideas. A teacher can encourage students to invest the time and energy necessary to solve nonroutine problems by:

1. providing an environment that encourages students to take intellectual risks and explore untested alternatives.

2. valuing all answers as potentially useful, but not all answers as equally useful.
3. praising persistence and unexpected solutions.
4. evaluating the quality of students' problem-solving efforts.
5. allowing group work during problem-solving sessions.
6. encouraging students to work on problems at home with their families.
7. establishing a systematic schedule for integrating problem-solving sessions into each strand of the mathematics curriculum.
8. introducing a systematic problem-solving plan.
9. asking appropriate questions during each problem-solving session.

A Four-step Problem-solving Plan

George Polya (1957) described a systematic problem-solving plan consisting of four interrelated steps:
- Understand the problem
- Select a strategy
- Carry out the strategy
- Evaluate the results

Teachers have used the four-step problem-solving plan summarized in the box on page 18 (Charles and Lester, 1982; Souviney, 1981). It is particularly helpful in solving nonroutine mathematics problems but can be used for routine word problems as well.

Step 1: Understand the Problem

The first step in solving a problem is to understand the information given in the problem statement and the intended goal. The following techniques have proven to be useful in helping students understand the problem situation and in selecting a solution strategy. Students can:

1. restate the problem in their own words.
2. use materials or sketches to model the problem situation.
3. make a list of all given facts.
4. make a list of the stated conditions and restrictions.
5. write the stated goal in their own words.
6. establish whether an exact or approximate answer is desired.
7. make a list of related information.
8. list unstated, or implicit, conditions.

9. Compare the current problem to problems solved previously.
10. Work with a partner or small group to discuss the problem.

Questions carefully posed by the teacher can stimulate student thinking during this phase in the problem-solving process. This is particularly true with young students and students who prefer verbalizing and role-playing problem situations.

Questions should promote critical thinking on the part of the students. Novice problem solvers should be encouraged to make conjectures, evaluate the ideas of others, and alter their positions in light of new evidence. An attempt to manufacture convincing arguments encourages students to look beyond the surface features stated in a problem statement and to explore the underlying mathematical structure and other associated conditions. It is rarely helpful for the teacher to provide specific answers at this point. It is far better for students to examine their own conjectures and discuss them with their peers. Appropriate questions might include:

1. What do you know about the problem?
2. Is it like any other problem you have solved?
3. What are some reasonable answers? Does the answer have to be exact? Could there be more than one correct answer?
4. Does your answer make sense? Can you convince me?
5. What can you do to find out?
6. What is wrong with that answer?

It is equally important for teachers to view the occurrence of incorrect answers and flawed reasoning as *opportunities* for learning. It is through the process of recognizing and attempting to repair inconsistencies in logic that students learn to question their current understanding of the problem situation.

The success of this approach depends to a great extent on how effectively the teacher can establish an atmosphere of acceptance for solving problems. Teachers should acknowledge all answers as appropriate for discussion. At this stage the student's persistence and the *quality* of an argument should be praised more than the accuracy and speed in achieving a solution.

FOUR-STEP PROBLEM-SOLVING PLAN

Step 1. Understand the Problem
- Relate given facts and conditions to problem goal
- Coordinate current problem with previously solved problems

Step 2. Select a Strategy
- Guess-and-Test
- Substitute Simpler or Extreme Values
- Divide Problem into Subtasks
- Work Backward
- Add an Element to the Problem Situation
- Reduce to a Simpler Case
- Conduct an Investigation
- Design a Model
- Draw a Sketch
- Make a Systematic List
- Make a Table
- Construct a Graph
- Search for a Pattern
- Construct a General Rule, Formula, or Function

Step 3. Carry Out the Strategy
- Persistently follow through with the solution strategy
- Maintain accurate records of the data collected
- Relate progress to steps 1 and 2

Step 4. Evaluate the Results
- If a solution is uncovered, refine results and relate them to other problems
- If not, reevaluate understanding and seek new solution strategy

Novices often find it helpful to work in pairs or groups of four. Students should also discuss the range of appropriate answers and the teacher can provide appropriate guidance at this point. For example, when asked for the population of the United States, an answer rounded to the nearest million persons is generally acceptable. However, for a smaller country such as Belize, a value rounded to, say, the nearest hundred thousand persons is expected. Questions of this type help students gain experience dealing with the complexity of the mathematical context for nonroutine problem solving. It is especially important for novice problem solvers to take time to explore and discuss the special features of each problem situation before pursuing the solution.

Step 2: Select a Strategy

Once the problem situation is well understood, a systematic solution strategy can be selected. Often novice problem solvers move prematurely to this step in the plan. This frequently results in a failure to identify key structural features of the problem situation itself, a necessary precursor to the selection of an effective solution strategy.

Encourage students to select a strategy based on past experience with related problems or on insight gathered from exploring the structure of the problem statement itself. One of the challenges for teachers is recognizing when to provide guidance at this stage and when to allow the struggle to continue unassisted. The teacher's task becomes one of recognizing the teaching moment and providing a level of guidance appropriate to the ability and experience of the learner. Polya (1957) suggested that questions and hints on selecting a solution strategy should be offered in such a manner that they could have occurred to the students themselves. Questions of this sort might include:

1. What are you trying to find?
2. What information is given?
3. What special conditions or restrictions apply?
4. Can you remember a previous problem with a similar goal? Could you use its solution to help in any way?
5. Can you restate the problem in your own words?
6. What are some possible and reasonable answers?
7. If you can't solve this problem, can you solve a similar one?
8. Did you use all the given information?
9. Is there unstated information that could be useful?
10. How do the stated conditions restrict the solution?

When mounting an assault on a novel problem, students have found the following arsenal of strategies to be useful. Many problems succumb to more than one approach, though often a wide range of problems may be solved through the judicious application of one favorite strategy. Following is a description of each strategy. Examples of problems solved by each strategy are included in the body of this book.

Guess-and-Test. This familiar trial-and-error technique can be used to solve a wide range of problems. Guess-and-test can be thought of as a preliminary, informal investigation motivated by pattern recognition and intuition. The solver makes an educated guess and then tests to see if the answer solves the problem. If it does not, the solver alters the guess according to the result and tests again until obtaining a satisfactory answer. Its simplicity makes the guess-and-test strategy well suited for elementary and middle-school students. What it gains in simplicity, however, it loses in efficiency. Generally, the guess-and-test method is more time-consuming than other strategies. It may, however, provide a critical initial insight into a problem situation.

Substitute Simpler or Extreme Values. Substituting less complex numbers for messy decimal and fractional values can make it easier for students to concentrate on the underlying structure of the problem or determine the correct operation(s) in story problems. The introduction of extreme values (very large or small) can sometimes help with testing one's understanding of the underlying assumptions associated with the problem situation. Once a solution path has been determined using the simpler substituted values, the original numbers can be reintroduced and the steps repeated.

Divide Problem into Subtasks. Students gain insight into some complex problems if the problems are separated into more manageable components. After carefully specifying two or more component problems, students can solve each in turn and combine the results to solve the original problem.

Work Backward. This strategy can be useful when the solution to a problem requires describing the systematic steps to achieve a known goal, or end state. To employ this strategy, one starts with the known end state and works backward to determine the sequence of steps, to reach the beginning state. Carrying out, or synthesizing, these steps in reverse will give the desired solution.

Add an Element to the Problem Situation.
A strategy often overlooked involves adding a new element to the problem situation in order to provide additional information to facilitate a solution.

Reduce to a Simpler Case. When a problem requires a long series of actions, it is often helpful to carefully document what happens in the first few steps of the process. Patterns discovered in these early stages can then be extrapolated to predict what will happen as the process continues.

Conduct an Investigation. Many complex, real-world problems in business, science, and engineering are addressed by conducting field investigations or carefully designed experiments. Elementary and middle-school students can also design and conduct investigations as a practical strategy for solving mathematics problems. Investigations require designing a physical representation of a problem situation. Students must learn to be systematic in carrying out an investigation. Sketches, lists, tables, and graphs can be used to organize data gathered from investigations. Once the results are organized, students can search for patterns that will help reveal the solution.

The remaining strategies are general tools that can be employed to help collect, organize, and analyze data in an investigation or experiment.

Design a Model. Sometimes it is impossible or dangerous to carry out an investigation by using the objects and reenacting events described in the problem situation. Designing a model that embodies the essential features of the problem situation may help lead to a solution.

Draw a Sketch. Drawing a sketch or diagram of a problem situation may help students visualize a solution.

Make a Systematic List. The solution to many problems result from the analysis of a careful listing of all possible outcomes.

Make a Table. Organizing data into a table can simplify the presentation of information and lead to the discovery of patterns and other clues to a solution.

Construct a Graph. Graphing information can result in a visual display that uncovers underlying relationships that might otherwise go unnoticed.

Search for a Pattern. Looking for numerical patterns in lists, tables, or graphs or for geometric patterns in a series of models or sketches often provides revealing clues to the structural relationships among elements of a problem that may lead to a solution.

Construct a General Rule. Analysis of a pattern in a table of results can lead to the construction of a general rule that systematically relates one element in the problem to another element. These rules can often be generalized to a mathematical function that can be used to solve a whole class of related problems.

Step 3: Carry Out the Strategy

Once the facts, conditions, and goals of a problem are understood, and a solution strategy has been selected, the next step is to apply the chosen strategy persistently. It should be noted that, in practice, steps 1, 2, and 3 are *not* independent activities. For example, in trying to understand a problem, one may find it useful to apply a favored strategy immediately to gather further information. This insight may lead to the selection of a more effective strategy.

Carrying out a solution requires persistence. The student's task is to determine whether or not the chosen strategy generates meaningful clues toward unraveling the problem. These clues may take the form of patterns that relate the problem to a previously solved example. When carrying out a strategy, novices should be encouraged to:

1. keep accurate records (tables, sketches, lists, graphs).
2. stick to their chosen strategy until some evidence suggests specific changes.
3. carefully monitor their thinking during each step in the solution.
4. if no progress is being made, put the problem aside for a day or so and then try it again.
5. select another strategy based on insight gained from initial attempt.

Step 4: Evaluate the Results

Once a problem is solved (or attempted without success), students should review the solution process. First, it provides an opportunity for learners to evaluate and refine their results. Second, it brings the process of solution into sharper focus. Students are better able to describe the intuitive processes immediately following a successful problem-solving experience. Students can evaluate the validity of their results, and more importantly, they can be encouraged to compare the current solution process with previously solved problems.

Once a successful solution has been found, students should:

1. describe, orally or in writing, the steps taken and the strategies employed in solving the problem.
2. discuss the form of the answer.
3. compare the problem and solution to previously solved problems.
4. solve extensions of the problem using the same strategy.
5. evaluate alternative solutions reported by peers.

ADAPTING INSTRUCTION FOR CHILDREN WITH SPECIAL NEEDS

Developing problem-solving skills is important for all children. While decision making, language usage, visual memory, and logical reasoning (all of which contribute to effective problem solving) are areas of difficulty for learning-disabled students, several techniques are available to help special-needs children learn to solve problems (Thornton & Bley, 1982).

Students who have difficulty reading can more easily participate in solving word problems that are recorded or presented orally. Students should also follow along with the recorded presentation using a printed narrative of the problem as a reference. To improve participation, you can present problem situations using pictures or graphics to help represent values or other elements of the problem. For example:

Mackenzie's mother bought 6 (🎁 🎁 🎁 🎁 🎁 🎁) prizes for the party.
She bought 4 (🎁 🎁 🎁 🎁) more the next day.
How many 🎁 did she buy altogether? _____

To help students understand what information is given in the problem narrative and what is needed to solve the problem, you can highlight key values and phrases using a colored marker. In this example, the bold type would be red:

Torin has **17** peanuts, and Rhiannon has **12**. Altogether, there are ____ **peanuts**.

As students gain experience, they can use markers to highlight key information in problems themselves. Different-colored markers can be used to highlight values and key phrases in two-step problems. In these examples, the bold type would be red and the italic type would be blue:

One quarter equals 25 cents.
A stack of *16 quarters is 1 inch tall*.
Bjorn is *50 inches tall*.
How much is a stack of quarters as tall as Bjorn worth?

1. *How many quarters equals Bjorn's height?*
   _____ quarters
2. **How much is the stack worth?**
   _____ cents _____ dollars

Students must first have a good understanding of the problem situation and the required mathematics operations. It is often helpful to review any arithmetic concepts involved in a problem before it is presented. For example, an initial worksheet might include exercises with answers and the student must insert the correct *operation*.

$$
\begin{array}{ccc}
35 & 34 & 315 \\
\square\,16 & \square\,9 & \square\,145 \\
\hline
19 & 306 & 460
\end{array}
$$

Like all young learners, learning-disabled students also need practice estimating answers as a way to check if solutions are reasonable. Predicting a reasonable answer before attempting a solution also helps students visualize the problem situation. As a warm-up activity, prepare a set of task cards that list possible estimated solutions for word problems. Have students select the most *reasonable* solution using only mental computation. For example:

Each Valentine card costs 22 cents.
Ethan has 31 classmates.
How much will Ethan spend to buy a card for
everyone in his class?
1.   *More than $5.00*
2.   *Less than $5.00*

Students then calculate each exercise and check
their solutions against their initial prediction.
Students can make up their own task cards using
problems from a textbook. Each task card should
list one reasonable estimate for the problem and
one or more poor solution estimates. Have the
class members exchange cards, determine the best
estimated solution for each problem, and check their
worked solutions against the estimate.

ASSESSMENT STRATEGY

Writing about problem solutions is a good way to
help students consolidate their thinking about their
work on a problem and share their results with
others. Younger students can report on their results
using sketches, labels, and symbols. For example,
the following six-step writing process was used by
Ford (1990) to help her third-grade students use
actual menus to calculate the cost of a family meal
at a restaurant. The students were asked to design
a problem that involved selecting items for a family
meal given a certain amount of money to spend.

- *Prewriting.* Students describe the age and
  number of family members and the amount of
  money they could spend and investigate copies
  of actual menus to determine possible meal
  items for individuals and items that could be
  shared.
- *Writing.* Each student writes a draft of a
  problem and tentative solution.
- *Conference.* Pairs of students read each other's
  problems and make suggestions on the form,
  completeness, and accuracy.
- *Revising and editing.* Each student makes
  corrections and produces a final draft.
- *Publication.* Each student carefully writes the
  problem on an index card with the solution
  on the back for publication in a class file box.
  Copies of menus are kept nearby.
- *Follow-up.* Students work each other's problems
  and discuss the solutions with the authors.

This procedure can be used with a wide range
of problems and grade levels and can be used as an
assessment activity as well. Written assignments such
as these can also be included in a student portfolio
and displayed on a problem bulletin board.

SAMPLE PROBLEM-SOLVING LESSON PLAN

The sample lesson plan on page 25 presupposes
that the students have already mastered necessary
computation skills or have access to a calculator to
facilitate the required arithmetic.

SUMMARY

- Problem solving is one of the important goals of
  mathematics instruction.
- A mathematical problem is a situation in which the
  context is readily understandable but no solution is
  immediately apparent.
- Students at all levels can successfully engage in
  problem-solving experiences.
- The two types of problems discussed were story
  problems and process problems.
- Story problems can be characterized as word
  problems that contain all the necessary
  information to affect a solution. Generally, the
  solver must identify one or more operations to
  carry out on the values given in the problem
  statement.
- Process problems are nonroutine situations
  that often require additional information or the
  reorganization of given facts in order to affect
  a solution. Strategies such as making a table,
  looking for patterns, and constructing general
  rules can be employed to solve process problems.
- Writing can often be used as an effective problem-
  solving tool.
- Generally, process problems can be solved in more
  than one way and may have multiple answers.
- Polya's four-step problem-solving plan can be
  employed by elementary students to solve routine
  word problems and nonroutine process problems.
- Specialized techniques can help special-needs
  children learn to solve mathematics problems.

LESSON TO INTRODUCE THE FOUR-STEP PROBLEM-SOLVING PLAN

Grade Level: Grades 6–7   Time Allotment: 50 minutes

NCTM Standard: Develop and apply a variety of strategies to solve problems, with emphasis on multistep and nonroutine problems.

Essential Understanding: Learning to solve nonroutine problems is an important component of mathematics study.

Goal: The learner will be able to apply a general problem-solving plan to nonroutine, multistep problems.

Objective: To introduce and practice using a general four-step problem-solving plan

Materials: A supply of twenty-five wooden blocks for each student; paper and pencil; overhead projector, blank transparency, and overhead pen.

Motivation: With the overhead projector turned off, build a five-step staircase of blocks (build the staircase flat on the surface of the overhead). A few inches to the right, build a ten-block stack (also flat on the surface of the overhead) that will be the tenth step and cover it with a piece of paper (leave enough space to insert steps 6–9 later). Turn on the overhead projector and ask the students what the construction looks like. Ask them to duplicate the staircase on their desks and to count the number of blocks required. Then remove the paper covering the tenth step and discuss how many total blocks it would take to make a ten-step staircase when steps 6–9 are included.

Procedure: Have the students mark off four sections on a piece of paper by dividing it in half vertically and horizontally (show an example on a transparency). Number the sections 1, 2, 3, and 4. Ask the students to write a description of the problem in section 1. Encourage them to use their own words. Have them include all the facts, unstated assumptions, and the problem goal. In section 2, have them list ways they may approach the problem (draw a picture, use the blocks, make a table, and so on). After everyone has written something in sections 1 and 2, have them begin to solve the problem. They will quickly find out that they do not have enough blocks and will need to try some other strategy. Have them use section 3 to show sketches, computations, and any notes about their progress. Walk around the room observing and posing questions and making comments such as, "Could drawing a sketch help?" or, "Maybe if you recorded your results in a table, it would be easier to keep track of your answers." Some students may decide to pool their blocks and solve the problem by constructing the ten-step staircase.

Assessment: After about fifteen minutes, have individuals tell the whole group how they attempted the solution. Have each child describe how he or she attempted to solve the problem in section 4. Make sure they explain why they think their answer is correct. Keep a record of individual student responses.

Extension Activity: Assign the problem of counting the number of blocks needed to construct a twenty-step staircase. Ask if anyone can find a way to predict the number of blocks needed for even larger staircases (e.g., fifty steps or one hundred steps). This would make a good homework project.

BIBLIOGRAPHY

Professional Articles

Ameis, J. (2004). How much water is in the skating rink? Mathematics Teaching in the Middle School, 10(4), 164–168.

Balka, D. (1988). Digit delight: Problem-solving activities using 0 through 9. *Arithmetic Teacher*, 36(3), 42–45.

Barson, A. (1985). And the last one loses! *Arithmetic Teacher*, 33(1), 35–37.

Bickerton-Ross, L. (1988). A practical experience in problem solving: A "10,000" display. *Arithmetic Teacher*, 36(4), 14–15.

Bitner, J., & Partridge, E. (1991). "Stocking up" on mathematics skills. *Arithmetic Teacher*, 38(7), 4–7.

Brown, S. (1990). Integrating manipulatives and computers in problem-solving experiences. *Arithmetic Teacher*, 36(2), 8–10.

Burns, M. (1985). The role of questioning. *Arithmetic Teacher*, 32(6), 14–16.

Burns, M. (1991). Introducing division through problem-solving experiences. *Arithmetic Teacher*, 38(8), 14–16.

Camen, P. (1989). Developing a problem-solving lesson. *Arithmetic Teacher*, 37(2), 14–19.

Carpenter, T. (1985). Research on the role of structure in thinking. *Arithmetic Teacher*, 32(6), 58–60.

Charles, R. (1981). Get the most out of "word problems." *Arithmetic Teacher*, 29(3), 39–40.

Charles, R. (1983). Evaluation and problem solving. *Arithmetic Teacher*, 30(5), 6–7.

Charles, R., & Martin, J. (1989). Steps toward building a successful problem-solving program. *Arithmetic Teacher*, 36(8), 25–26.

Cobb, P., Yackel, E., Wood, T., Wheatley, G., & Merkel, G. (1988). Creating a problem solving atmosphere. *Arithmetic Teacher*, 36(1), 46–47.

Dougherty, B., & Tucker, S. (1989). Applying number sense to problem solving. *Arithmetic Teacher*, 36(6), 22–25.

Fennell, F., & Ammon, R. (1985). Writing techniques for problem solvers. *Arithmetic Teacher*, 33(1), 24–25.

Ford, M. (1990). The writing process: A strategy for problem solvers. *Arithmetic Teacher*, 38(3), 35–38.

Frank, M. (1988). Problem solving and mathematical beliefs. *Arithmetic Teacher*, 35(5), 32–34.

Fortunato, I., Hecht, D., Tittle, C., & Alvarez, L. (1991). Metacognition and problem solving. *Arithmetic Teacher*, 39(4), 38–40.

Gilbert-Macmillan, K., & Leitz, S. (1986). Cooperative small groups: A method for teaching problem solving. *Arithmetic Teacher*, 33(7), 9–11.

Kroll, D., Masingila, J., & Mau, S. (1992). Cooperative problem solving: But what about grading?. *Arithmetic Teacher*, 39(6), 17–23.

LeBlanc, J. (1982). Teaching textbook story problems. *Arithmetic Teacher*, 29(6), 52–54.

Matz, K., & Leier, C. (1992). Word problems and the language connection. *Arithmetic Teacher*, 39(8), 14–17.

Mathematical Thinking Focus Issue. (1985). *Arithmetic Teacher*, 33(6).

McGivney-Burelle, J. (2005). Connecting the dots: Network problems that foster mathematical thinking. *Teaching Children Mathematics*, 11(5), 272–277.

Moses, B. (1982). Individual differences in problem solving. *Arithmetic Teacher*, 30(4), 10–14.

Moyer, M., & Moyer, J. (1985). Ensuring that practice makes perfect: Implications for children with learning disabilities. *Arithmetic Teacher*, 33(1), 40–42.

Ponce, G., & Garrison, L. (2005). Overcoming the "walls" surrounding word problems. *Teaching Children Mathematics*, 11(5), 256–260.

Problem Solving Focus Issue. (1978). *Arithmetic Teacher*, 33(1).

Rosenbaum, L., Behounek, K., Brown, L., & Burcalow, J. (1989). Step into problem solving with cooperative learning. *Arithmetic Teacher*, 36(7), 7–11.

Sanfiorenzo, N. (1991). Evaluating expressions: A problem-solving approach. *Arithmetic Teacher*, 38(7), 34–38.

Scharton, S. (2004). I did it my way. *Arithmetic Teacher*, 10(5), 278–283.

Szetela, W. (1987). The problem of evaluation in problem solving: Can we find a solution. *Arithmetic Teacher*, 35(3), 36–41.

Talton, C. (1988). Let's solve the problem before we find the answer. *Arithmetic Teacher*, 36(1), 40–45.

Thornton, C., & Bley, S. (1982). Problem solving: Help in the right direction for LD students. *Arithmetic Teacher*, 29(6), 26–27, 38–41.

Woodward, E. (1991). Problem solving in the preservice classroom. *Arithmetic Teacher*, 39(3), 41–43.

Yackel, E., & Cobb, P. (1994). The development of young children's understanding of mathematical argumentation. Paper presented at the annual meeting of the American Educational Research Association, New Orleans.

Yancey, A., Thompson, C., & Yancey, J. (1989). Step into problem solving with cooperative learning. *Arithmetic Teacher*, 36(7), 15–19.

Additional References and Readings

Bell, E., & Bell, R. (1985). Writing and mathematical problem solving: Arguments in favor of synthesis. *School Science and Mathematics*, 85(3), 210–221.

Brown, J., & Burton, R. (1978). Diagnostic models for procedural bugs in basic mathematics skills. *Cognitive Science*, 2, 155–192.

Burns, M. (1977a). *The good time math event book*. Palo Alto, CA: Creative Publications.

Burns, M. (1977b). *I hate math*. New York: Little, Brown.

Burns, M. (1978). *The book of think*. New York: Little, Brown.

Burns, M. (1987). *A collection of math lessons*. New Rochelle, NY: Cuisenaire Company of America.

Butts, T. (1980). Posing problems properly. In S. Krulik & R. Reys (Eds.), *Problem solving in school mathematics: 1980 yearbook* (pp. 23–33). Reston, VA: National Council of Teachers of Mathematics.

Charles, R., & Lester, F. (1982). *Teaching problem solving: What, why and how*. Palo Alto, CA: Dale Seymour.

Chi, M., Feltovich, P., & Glasser, R. (1981). Characterization and representation of physics problems by experts and novices. *Cognitive Science*, 5, 121–152.

Curcio, F. (Ed.). (1987). *Teaching and learning: A problem-solving focus*. Reston, VA: National Council of Teachers of Mathematics.

Dudeney, E. (1966). *The Canterbury puzzles*. New York: Dover.

Erlwanger, S. (1975). Case studies of children's conceptions of mathematics (Part 1). *Journal of Children's Mathematical Behavior, Summer*.

Gardner, M. (Ed.). (1952). *Mathematical puzzles of Sam Loyd*. New York: Dover.

Gardner, M. (1956). *Mathematics, magic and mystery*. New York: Dover.

Gardner, M. (1966). *Mathematical puzzles and diversions*. New York: Dover.

Ginsburg, H. (1983). *The developmental of mathematical thinking*. New York: Academic Press.

Greenes, C., Spungin, R., & Dombrowski, J. (1977). *Problem-mathics: Mathematical challenge problems with solution strategies*. Palo Alto, CA: Creative Publications.

Holtzman, C., & Bresser, R. (1999). *Developing number sense: Grades 3–6*. Sausalito, CA: Math Solutions Publications.

Jacobs, H. (1970). *Mathematics: A human endeavor*. San Francisco: W. H. Freeman.

Krulik, S., & Reys, R. (Ed.). (1980). *Problem solving in school mathematics: 1980 Yearbook*. Reston, VA: National Council of Teachers of Mathematics.

Krutetskii, V. (1976). *The psychology of mathematics abilities in school children*. Chicago: University of Chicago Press.

Lesh, R., & Landan, M. (Eds.). (1983). *The acquisition of mathematical concepts and processes*. New York: Academic Press.

Mehan, H., Miller-Souviney, B., Riel, M., Souviney, R., Whooley, K., & Liner, B. (1986). *The write help*. Glenview, IL: Scott, Foresman.

Meiring, S. (1980). *Problem solving—A basic mathematics goal*. Columbus: Ohio Department of Education.

O'Daffer, P. (Ed.). (1988). *Problem solving tips for teachers*. Reston, VA: National Council of Teachers of Mathematics.

Polya, G. (1957). *How to solve it*. Princeton: Princeton University Press.

Polya, G. (1962). *Mathematical discovery; On understanding, learning, and teaching problem solving*. New York: John Wiley.

Seymour, D., Holmberg, V., & Laycock, M. (1973). *Aftermath*. Palo Alto, CA: Creative Publications.

Seymour, D., & Shedd, M. (1973). *Finite differences: A problem solving technique*. Palo Alto, CA: Creative Publications.

Shoenfeld, A. (1985). *Mathematical problem solving*. Orlando, FL: Academic Press.

Silver, E. (1979). Student perceptions of relatedness around mathematical verbal problems. *Journal for Research in Mathematics Education*, 10, 195–210.

Souviney, R. (1977). *Recreational mathematics*. *Learning Magazine*, May, 55–56.

Souviney, R. (1979). *Math problems—Life problems*. *Teacher Magazine*, February, 49–51.

Souviney, R. (1981). *Solving problems kids care about*. Glenview, IL: Scott, Foresman.

Suydam, M. (1980). Untangling clues from research on problem solving. In *Problem solving in school mathematics: 1980 Yearbook* (pp. 34–50). Reston, VA: National Council of Teachers of Mathematics.

Wertheimer, M. (1959). *Productive thinking*. New York: Harper & Row.

Wirtz, R. (1976). *Banking on problem solving*. Washington, DC: Curriculum Development Associates.

Section II

Teaching Strategies for Mathematical Problem Solving

Chapter 3
Whole-class Problem-solving Warm-ups

BREAKING INTO GROUPS-OF-FOUR

Present the problem of dividing the class into groups-of-four with each student having an equal chance of being in any group. In a teacher-directed large-group discussion, have the class brainstorm possible random selection techniques and then discuss the effects of each suggestion. Start by listing all the suggestions on the board without comment. Then, the class should discuss each suggestion and choose the most effective methods.

Some possible suggestions for a class of thirty-two include:

1. Deal out an appropriate-sized, shuffled deck of cards and form groups of people with the same number.
2. Alphabetize the class list and count off by fours.
3. Draw names out of a hat, four at a time.
4. Have students draw out of a hat containing four sets of cards numbered 1 through 8. Those with the same number go together.

BRAINSTORMING

Have the whole class work together to "brainstorm" possible answers, using questions similar to those below. Write responses on a piece of posterboard or on the blackboard. Discuss each response in detail, making sure everyone has an opportunity for input.

1. Name ten things that come in millions.
2. Name ten things that you can do with a blade of grass.
3. If you had to leave home quickly and could only take one suitcase with you, what would you put in it?
4. This school would be a better place if everyone…

5. Name ten things you can do with a pencil sharpener.
6. List ten words that describe this class.
7. List ten things you can do now that you couldn't do last year.
8. Make up an interesting question for the class to brainstorm.

MIND READING

Ask each student in your class to think of a number between 1 and 50. Both digits must be odd and they cannot be alike. For example, you cannot use 11. Have each student secretly write his or her number on a piece of paper.

Before starting the activity, secretly write the number 37 on the board and cover it with a piece of paper. After the whole class has written down its guesses, ham it up a bit, asking them to concentrate on their numbers so you can read their minds. Dramatically remove the paper covering the number on the board and ask how many students chose the number 37. A surprising number of students will probably have chosen this number.

Try the same activity again, but ask for a number between 50 and 100 made up of two different even digits. This time write the digits 6 and 8 on two large cards (or use playing cards). Again ask them to concentrate, and then show them the number 68. Many will have chosen this number. Reverse the cards and explain that they may have gotten their wires crossed if they chose 86.

Though this seems like a magic act, in fact there are only eight numbers that fit the first category and for some curious psychological reason, most people choose 37 (the next most popular number is 35). The second situation is restricted to eight choices as well, with 68 being the most popular. Of course, reversing the cards to show 86 thereby increases your mind-reading success.

RACE TO 21

Race to 21 is played by two people taking turns counting one or two numbers until someone reaches 21. Chose who is to start. The first person can either say "1" or "1, 2." The other contestant counts on from where the first person left off (again saying one or two numbers). This process of alternate counting continues until reaching 21. The winner is the person who says 21. This game can be played with all ages and various-sized groups. The teacher should play against volunteers in the class to help students learn the counting procedure. Then have the children pair off and see if they can develop a winning strategy.

A clever way to unravel this problem is to play the game backward. If you want to say 21, which previous number must you say? If you say 18, your opponent could count "19," or "19, 20." Either way, you could claim 21. If you must say 18, which previous number must you say? This time 15 is the key number, because saying it guarantees you can claim 18. Continue this process. If you say 3, you are guaranteed all the key numbers to 21. To say by 3, your opponent must start (unless you are very lucky). However, if you have been chosen to start, try to capture a key number as soon as possible. Once you say a multiple of 3, you are guaranteed to be a winner (if you don't make any mistakes).

Once your students have mastered this version, try counting one, two, or three numbers at a time. Another interesting twist is to make 21 "poison"— the person who says 21 loses.

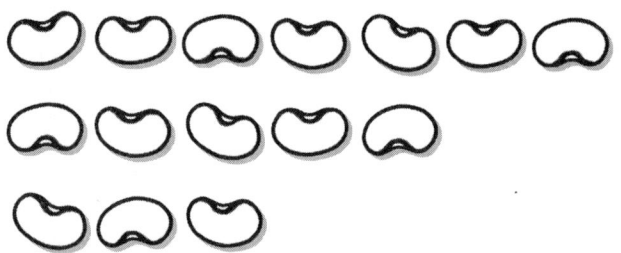

Warm-up NIM Game

WARM-UP NIM GAME

Rules: Two players take turns removing one or more counters from any one row. Each player may remove counters from only one row on each turn but may switch to another row on the next turn. The player who removes the last of the counters wins.

The NIM game-winning parity strategy was discussed in chapter 2. Players quickly discover that if they can leave their opponent faced with two equal rows (a state of parity), they can always win. The more complicated strategy of mentally grouping the counters in each row by powers-of-2 and looking for states of parity can be used to win any NIM-type game.

After students learn to win three-row NIM, have them use their strategies to play four-row NIM by adding one more counter as a fourth row.

Four-row 7/5/3/1 NIM Game

Introduce this activity several times to your class and have students play different partners to encourage different parity strategies. Once they have completely solved three- and four-row NIM, students can try different starting configurations (i.e., 9/7/5/3/1 or 7/7/5/5/1) and test if they can use the base-2 parity strategy to give them the winning advantage.

PICO-FERMI-NADA

The goal of Pico-Fermi-Nada is to guess a secret three-digit number. The leader writes any three-digit number on a piece of paper and hides it. Individuals or teams take turns guessing three-digit numbers. Each time someone guesses, the leader gives one of the clues below:

1. Pico—At least one digit is correct and in the correct position.
2. Fermi—At least one digit is correct but is in the wrong position.
3. Nada—No digits are correct.

Try to guess the secret number in the fewest possible attempts. Teams can play against each other, alternating guesses and learning the clues from each other. The whole class can also play as a unit trying to reduce the number of guesses from one trial to the next.

Here is a sample game: Secret number 714.

	Guess	Clue—Comments
1	987	Fermi—At least one digit correct but in wrong position.
2	999	Nada—No digit correct (9 is not a digit in the secret number).
3	888	Nada—No digit correct (8 is not a digit in the secret number).
4	978	Fermi—7 is a correct digit but must be in the first position.
5	654	Pico—At least one digit is correct (6 is not a digit in the secret number).
6	235	Nada—2, 3, and 5 are not digits in the secret number.
7	714	Pico, Pico, Pico—Guesser could have guessed 704 or 764, requiring additional clues.

The comments in this table provide examples of logical deductions students can make after each guess and clue. With experience, students can carefully choose guesses to provide as much information as possible from each of the clues. With practice, students can "guess" any three-digit number in seven to ten tries.

CAR RACE

Show your class how to graph coordinate pairs before playing Car Race. Beginning at (0,0) on the following coordinating graph, explain that the first number in the pair (3,4) tells you to go right three spaces and the second tells you to go up four spaces. The car shows you where to end up.

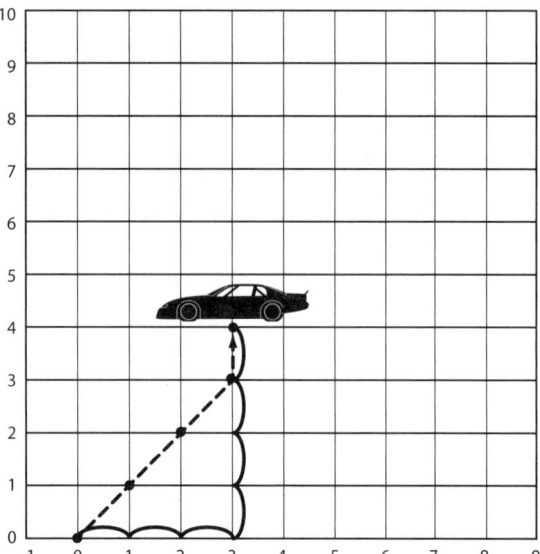

To play Car Race, draw a wide, curved road on a piece of 1-cm grid paper. Each player begins at the starting line. For example, three racers could start at (-1, 0), (0,0) and (1,0). To race, each player in turn can add (or subtract) 1 from his/her first and/or second coordinate and move his/her car to the spot indicated by the new coordinate pair. (Avoid negative numbers until the class decides they need them later in the problem. See the following example.) After everyone has moved once, again add (or subtract) 1 to either or both coordinates and move on from the last position. Continue adding (or subtracting) 1 to each subsequent move and try to negotiate the curves without crashing into the edge of the road or another car. The first one to the finish line without crashing is the winner.

Begin by having the whole class race one car. Later, break into groups of two or three and have the students work on efficient strategies by racing against each other.

Help students notice that each time 1 is added to one of the coordinates, the car moves ahead and can also change direction. Subtracting 1 has the opposite effect. Continue adding (or subtracting) 1 on each subsequent move. They should try to negotiate the

curves without crashing into the edge of the road or another car. They should also be careful not to get too close to the edge or they won't be able to turn in time to avoid a crash. Students can play a few practice games and see if they can get to the finish line without a mishap. Whoever gets there first wins. To make the game more realistic, allow players to increment 1 or 2 units on the x-axis or y-axis for each move.

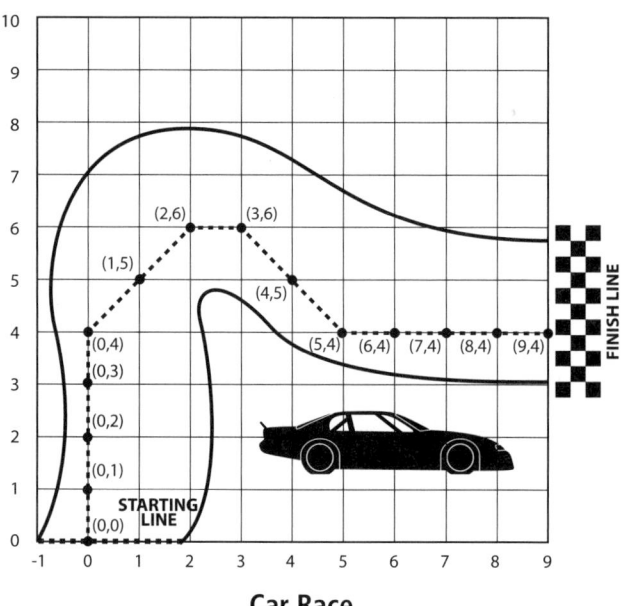

Car Race

RACE MOVES

Horizontal Change	Position	Vertical Change
	(0.0)	
NC	(0,1)	+1
NC	(0,2)	+1
NC	(0,3)	+1
NC	(0,4)	+1
+1	(1,5)	+1
+1	(2,6)	+1
+1	(3,6)	NC
+1	(4,5)	-1
+1	(5,4)	-1
+1	(6,4)	NC
+1	(7,4)	NC
+1	(8,4)	NC
+1	(9,4)	NC

NC= No Change

Chapter 4
Problems and Solutions

FIND THAT HOMEWORK
(Problem Starter Sheet 1, page 97)
Before excusing the class, the teacher said that their assignment that night was to "find" their homework. She said that the homework assignment was on two facing pages in their textbook, and the sum of the two page numbers equaled 65. What homework pages were assigned?

Solution: Find That Homework
Understand the Problem
Facts
- Looking at any book, notice that facing pages are always numbered with an even page number on the left and an odd page number on the right.
- Homework page numbers must be consecutive values.

Conditions
- The homework pages must be between 2 and 65.
- Sum of the two consecutive page numbers must equal exactly 65.

Goal
- Find the homework page numbers.

Select a Strategy
First, students should try guessing a possible answer and see how close they are to 65. If they are low, they can pick two larger consecutive page numbers, and if they are high, they can pick two lower consecutive page numbers and compare the sum to the goal.

Carry Out the Strategy
They should pick two facing page numbers and compute the sum (e.g., 24 + 25 = 49). Because the answer is too small, they should make the second guess larger (e.g., 40 + 41 = 81). Because this result is too large, the answer must be between the two guesses. Additional thoughtful guesses will narrow the range of possible solutions, eventually yielding the answer (32 + 33 = 65).

Evaluate the Results
The homework is on pages 32 and 33 because this is the only pair of consecutive numbers that equal 65 and the first number is even, as is required for facing pages in a book. We could have made a better initial guess if we realized that the page numbers were about half of 65 because there were two of them (i.e., 65 ÷ 2 = 32.5). Students might notice the pattern of sums for two consecutive whole numbers. Because an odd number is always the next lower even number plus 1, an even number plus an odd number equals an even number plus an even number plus 1, which is itself an odd number (i.e., even + odd = even + even + 1 = odd). Therefore, the sum of facing page numbers must always be odd. What would be the answer to a homework assignment if the teacher assigned two facing pages with page numbers equal to 100? (49+51 are not facing pages so there is no homework tonight!)

Using the same logic, you can be sure that when you add three consecutive numbers, you have two possible outcomes: One odd and two even numbers give an odd sum, and two odd and one even number give an even sum. If the teacher assigned three pages of homework, then we could initially try numbers about one-third of 65 (20 + 21 + 22 = 63 and 21 + 22 + 23 = 66). So there would be no pages of homework if the teacher assigned three pages equal to 65.

Problem and Solution 2

TOOTH TRUTHS
(Problem Starter Sheet 2, page 98)
Which grade level in your school is missing the most teeth? Fill in the table to help you find out.

Teacher	Grade	Missing Teeth

Solution: Tooth Truths
Understand the Problem
  Facts
  - Little kids lose a lot of teeth in primary school.

  Conditions
  - Assume that the number of missing teeth averages out about the same over the whole year for any grade level.

  Goal
  - Find out which grade level is missing the most teeth.

Select a Strategy
Have groups of students interview children in other classrooms and collect data on the number of missing teeth. Keep track of the grade levels as well. Compile all the data on a chart or the blackboard.

Carry Out the Strategy
Arrange with the other teachers to expect "visitors" at a specified time. Students in small groups should record the tooth facts on their tables and return to their class for a large-group discussion. (Don't forget to count missing teeth in your own class.) Arrange the resut for each grade level and graph the results on a classroom chart to make comparisons easier.

Evaluate the Results
The results will vary somewhat according to the time of year, but when the number of missing teeth is averaged by grade level, the first grade should come out ahead. The graph should help your class make comparisons across classes. You should discuss the need to sample groups of equal size if the comparisons are to be meaningful. Clearly, if you interview twice as many second graders as first graders, the resulting graph will be misleading.

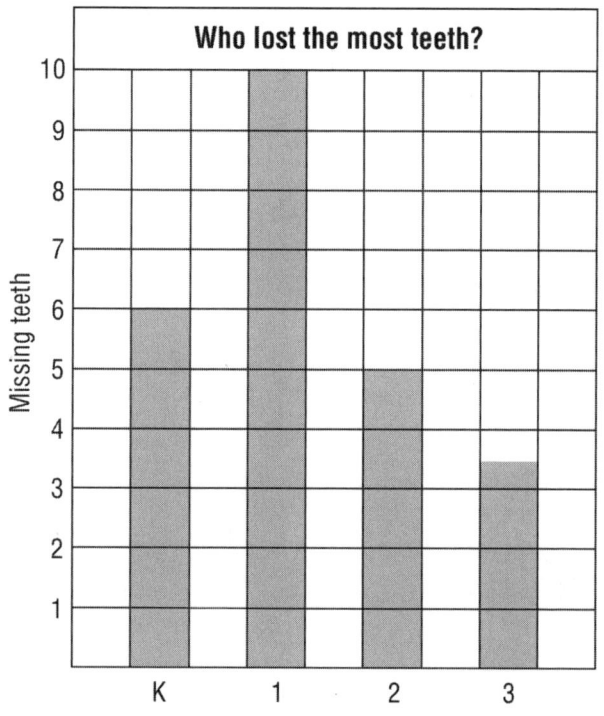

Problem and Solution 3

FRUIT FACTS

(Problem Starter Sheet 3, page 99)
Oranges are a famous fruit first found in China. They come in many sizes and colors. Some have thick skins, some thin. Some are sweet while others are bitter. Do all oranges have the same number of sections? How many seeds are in an orange? Does it matter if they are big or small? See if you can find out.

Solution: Fruit Facts

Understand the Problem

Facts
- There are many types of oranges.

Conditions
- All oranges may not have the same number of seed or sections. Try different types and sizes.

Goal
- Find out how many seeds and sections are in an orange.

Select a Strategy

Much can be learned about the characteristics and uses of oranges by talking with the local grocer. It is important as well for students to begin utilizing the learning resources available throughout the community. If students have oranges in their lunches, have them conduct an experiment by carefully peeling their oranges and counting the seeds and sections.

Carry Out the Strategy

This part will vary from region to region. However, encourage your students to actually visit the supermarket and talk with produce people. The results of the experiment should show that small and large oranges of the same type have the same number of sections, though the seed count will vary somewhat. Our last orange had thirteen sections and six seeds.

Evaluate the Results

Perhaps the most important result is for your students to begin seeing other people in the community as learning resources. The grocer, the mechanic, and the hairdresser all have a math story to tell you if you just know the right questions to ask.

It is interesting to note that there are many right answers, depending on the type of orange. Other factors such as what constitutes a whole section or how big does a seed have to be to count is the stuff engineering problem solvers work with daily. Try making a classroom graph by gluing the seeds on a piece of posterboard as shown below.

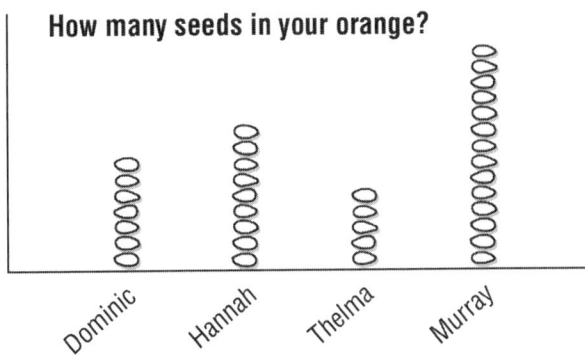

How many seeds in your orange?

With a bit of imagination, you can come up with a whole series of fruit problems to give meaning to those rainy-day classroom lunches.

Problem and Solution 4

MYSTERY MASSES

(Problem Starter Sheet 4, page 100)

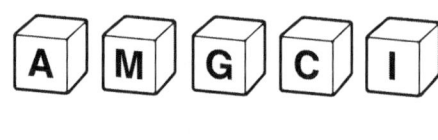

Put the boxes in order from lightest to heaviest. Below, write the mystery word the boxes spell:

Light   Heavy

Solution: Mystery Masses

Teacher Note: Using five identical boxes (35 mm slide boxes work well), prepare the mystery masses by putting varying amounts of sand in each. Make sure there is a sufficient difference in mass to tip the scale for any pair of boxes. Order the boxes from light to heavy and letter the boxes M A G I C. Mix them up on the table and set small groups to work with the pan balance.

Understand the Problem
Facts
- Five identical boxes are each filled with a different amount of sand.
Conditions
- Use only a pan balance to help with comparisons.
Goal
- Order the boxes from light to heavy and spell out the mystery word.

Select a Strategy
Compare the mass of any pair. Set the light one aside and continue with the other four until you have determined the heaviest. Repeat the process with the four remaining boxes and so on until you have all the boxes in order.

Carry Out the Strategy
Here are the results of the first cycle of comparisons:

Therefore, *C* is the heaviest. The next cycle might give these results:

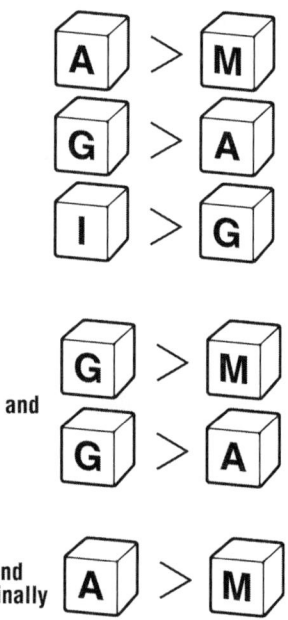

Therefore, *I* is the next heaviest, then *G, A,* and *M.*

Evaluate the Results
The mystery word is M A G I C. It is possible to order a set of five objects in $4 + 3 + 2 + 1 = 10$ comparisons. How many comparisons would it take for six objects? Seven? Have your class bring in identical small containers (one-serving cereal boxes or ½-pint milk cartons) and construct their own set of mystery masses. Have them letter the boxes with a favorite word or name and give to a friend to solve.

Problem and Solution 5

APPLE SHARING
(Problem Starter Sheet 5, page 101)
Share an apple so that you and your two friends get the same amount.

How many seeds are in the apple?

Do all apples have the same number of seeds?

Put the seeds in the sun for a few days. Plant them and see what happens.

You will need:

You

Two friends

One apple

Solution: Apple Sharing
Understand the Problem
Facts
- There are three people and one apple.

Conditions
- You can cut the apple into as many pieces as desired.

Goal
- Divide the apple into three equal amounts, so everyone is happy with his or her share. Count the number of seeds and determine if all apples have the same number.

Select a Strategy
Each person takes a turn cutting the apple into three equal quantities. There may be lots of little pieces. The last person to cut the apple also chooses last.

To find out if all apples have the same number of seeds, students should talk with the grocer (have them try interviewing different ones in the community) and check the number of seeds in several types of apples. Dry the seeds and plant them.

Carry Out the Strategy
The process of dividing into thirds should be tried by several groups of three and discussed. When counting seeds, students should keep a record in a table as below:

TYPE OF APPLE	NUMBER OF SEEDS
1. Red Delicious	9
2.	
3.	
4.	

Evaluate the Results
This set of open-ended problems gives children an opportunity to see that problems can sometimes be solved better cooperatively. Also in this process, the concept of one-third is developed.

The seed problem offers additional practice observing, organizing, and predicting, all of which are important in our everyday lives. Children may also come to appreciate the knowledge other members of the community have to offer and consequently seek them out as learning resources.

Our most recent apple had nine seeds. Our experience has shown that the number for various types of eating apples does not vary greatly from this sample. We have had mixed results planting apple seeds. Try drying enough seeds so each student can plant three or four. If you're lucky and the seeds are carefully taken care of, some should sprout.

Problem and Solution 6

CLAY BOATS

(Problem Starter Sheet 6, Page 102)

Can you make a clay boat that floats?

Try it.

See how many marbles it will carry.

You will need:

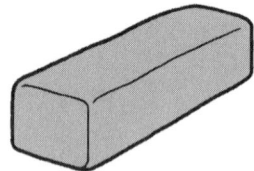

Clay

Pail of water

Marbles

Solution: Clay Boats

Understand the Problem

   Facts

- Use a piece of modeling clay.

   Conditions

- Everyone uses the same amount of clay.

   Goal

- Make a clay boat that floats and see how many marbles it will carry.

Select a Strategy

Using a trial-and-error strategy, have each student "pinch" out a boat and try to float it in a pail of water. Stop periodically to discuss partial or complete successes. Once everyone has a boat floating, distribute marbles to see which boat can "float" the most marbles.

Carry Out the Strategy

Discussing success throughout the trial-and-error period should help shape future designs and make the whole process more efficient. Fundamentally, this group problem-solving process got us to the moon.

Evaluate the Results

Given time and encouragement, most children will construct a "floater." More efficient boats will have thin walls and maximum interior volumes. Half of a sphere is the most effective shape and should carry the most marbles.

Problem and Solution 7

COOL COSTS

(Problem Starter Sheet 7, page 103)
It takes more gas to run a car with the air conditioner turned on than with it off. (If you open the windows when the air conditioner is off, however, there may not be much difference in the mileage due to the wind resistance caused by the open windows.) The table below shows the miles per gallon of gasoline for a car with and without the air conditioner running. How much extra will it cost to run the air conditioner for a 4-hour, 45-minute trip at 55 miles per hour if gasoline costs $2.09 per gallon?

MILEAGE WITH AND WITHOUT AIR CONDITIONING (A/C)

	Speed in MPH				
	40	45	50	55	60
Without air conditioning	34	33	31	29	26
With air conditioning	32	31	28	26	22

Solution: Cool Costs

Understand the Problem

Facts
- Gasoline costs $2.09 per gallon.
- The trip took 4 hours and 45 minutes.
- The speed of the car was 55 miles per hour.

Conditions
- The windows were rolled up whether the air conditioner was on or off.
- The road was flat, because going up and down hills might change the mileage table.

Goal
- Determine the cost of running the air conditioner in this car.

Select a Strategy

It is easier to start with simple values, which will help students to more easily work out the appropriate calculation procedures. Then they can go back and substitute the actual values and calculate the correct answer.

Carry Out the Strategy

Start students with the assumption that the trip took 5 hours and that gasoline cost $2 per gallon. In 5 hours traveling at 55 miles per hour, the car would travel 5 x 55 = 275 miles, or about 300 miles. If the car got 30 miles per gallon (the table shows 29, but let's continue to use simple numbers), the 5-hour trip would require about 300 ÷ 30 = 10 gallons of gasoline, costing a total of 10 x $2 = $20. Now use the same calculations but substitute the actual values:

4 hours & 45 minutes = 4.75 hours
    (note 45 minutes = 3/4 hour = .75 hour)
4.75 x 55 = 261.25 miles
261.25 ÷ 29 = 9.01 gallons (without A/C)
261.25 ÷ 26 = 10.05 gallons (with A/C)
9.01 x $2.09 = $18.83 (without A/C)
10.05 x $2.09 = $21.01 (with A/C)

Evaluate the Results

The extra cost of running the air conditioner for the entire trip was $2.18, and therefore about $0.46 per hour to run the air conditioner at 55 mph in this car ($2.18 ÷ 4.75 = .46). Using the mileage chart, you can calculate the cost of gasoline and how much the air conditioning costs change as a result of increased or decreased speed.

Problem and Solution 8

CHANGING CHANGE

(Problem Starter Sheet 8, page 104)
How many ways can you make change for 16¢?

Solution: Changing Change

Understand the Problem

Facts

- Use dimes, nickels, and pennies.

Conditions

- You do not need to use all three types of coins each time.

Goal

- Find all the ways to make change for 16¢.

Select a Strategy

Using make-believe or real money, find a combination of coins equaling 16¢ using the largest coins first. Record the results in the table. Continue making new combinations, always using the largest possible until you reach sixteen pennies. Some children may find it easier to draw the coins instead of recording the results numerically.

Carry Out the Strategy

The table below lists all the ways to make change for 16¢.

Evaluate the Results

There are six ways to make 16¢ using dimes, nickels, and pennies. This activity gives students practice with systematically searching for all possible combinations. It is a very difficult task for many young children to locate all the combinations and know when they have finished. After individuals or groups have worked on the problem, a whole-class discussion is in order.

More complex money problems can be posed by increasing the total amount slightly. There are nine ways to make 21¢ and 782 ways to make $1.21! (See Money Matters, page 64.) Limit the types of coins or total amounts in order to keep the number of combinations reasonable.

CHANGE FOR 16¢

	10¢	5¢	1¢	
1	1 dime	1 nickel	1 penny	=16¢
2	1	0	6	=16¢
3	0	3	1	=16¢
4	0	2	6	=16¢
5	0	1	11	=16¢
6	0	0	16	=16¢

Problem and Solution 9

CANDY BARS

(Problem Starter Sheet 9, page 105)
Here are some whole candy bars:

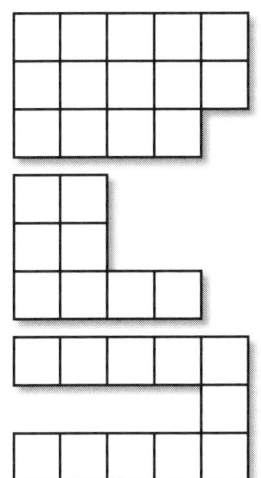

Here are some whole candy bars with bites out of them. These are not whole candy bars.

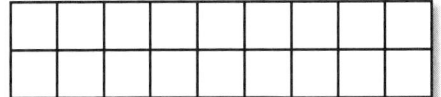

No candy bar can have more than 9 units on an edge.

How many different whole candy bars can you make?

Solution: Candy Bars

Understand the Problem

Facts
- Candy bars are rectangular arrays of small squares with no bites out of them.
- A (2,3) candy bar is considered the same as a (3,2) candy bar.

Conditions
- No candy bar can be larger than 9 units on any edge.

Goal
- Find the total number of different candy bars.

Select a Strategy

Using 1-cm grid paper, cut out all possible candy bars from 1 to 9 units on an edge. Use a systematic procedure to ensure that no candy bars are skipped. Keep in mind that just rotating a candy bar does not make it different. For example, the candy bars below are not different.

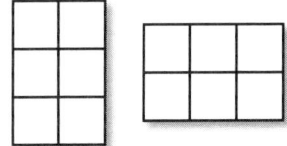

Record the results in a table to make it easy to count the total number of candy bars.

Carry Out the Strategy

The table below shows all possible candy bars with 1 to 9 units on an edge.

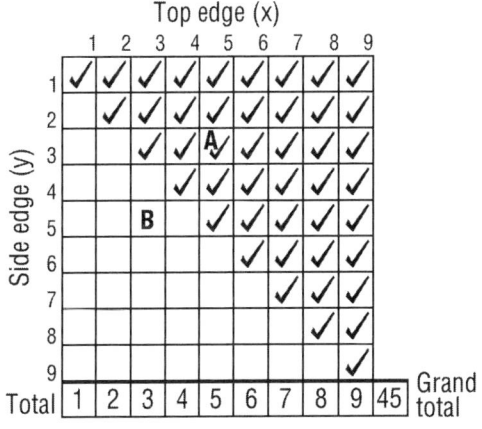

				Top edge (x)					
Side edge (y)	1	2	3	4	5	6	7	8	9
1	✓	✓	✓	✓	✓	✓	✓	✓	✓
2		✓	✓	✓	✓	✓	✓	✓	✓
3			✓	✓	A✓	✓	✓	✓	✓
4				✓	✓	✓	✓	✓	✓
5				B		✓	✓	✓	✓
6						✓	✓	✓	✓
7							✓	✓	✓
8								✓	✓
9									✓
Total	1	2	3	4	5	6	7	8	9

Grand total: 45

Teacher Note: The check marks indicate a candy bar of length (x) and height: (3,5) = A. Notice that only the top part of the table is filled in with check marks. The unchecked boxes correspond to the rotated candy bars: (5, 3) = B. The number of checks in each column is totaled at the bottom and the grand total is shown on the right.

Evaluate the Results

There are exactly 45 different candy bars with edges 1 to 9 units in length. An interesting extension of this problem involves finding a pattern for the number of possible candy bars using different maximum edge lengths. The table below lists the results of several experiments using maximum edge lengths of 1 through 9.

Maximum Edge Length	Pattern		Number of Candy Bars
1	1	=	1
2	1+2	=	3
3	1+2+3	=	6
4	1+2+3+4	=	10
5	1+2+3+4+5	=	15
6	1+2+3+4+5+6	=	21
7	1+2+3+4+5+6+7	=	28
8	1+2+3+4+5+6+7+8	=	36
9	1+2+3+4+5+6+7+8+9	=	45

A clear pattern is evident. The total number of candy bars with a maximum of 20 units on an edge should be $1 + 2 + 3 + \ldots + 20 = 210$ candy bars. Some of your students may enjoy trying to figure out a shortcut for adding all those numbers together, especially for large candy bars (i.e., 1,000 on an edge). Notice that by writing the series $1 + 2 + 3 + 4 + 5 + 6 + 7 + 8 + 9 + 10$ as below and adding pairs, we get a total of five elevens or $5 \times 11 = 55$. Does this pattern always work?

$$
\begin{array}{ccccc}
1 & 2 & 3 & 4 & 5 \\
+ \quad 10 & 9 & 8 & 7 & 6 \\
\hline
11 & 11 & 11 & 11 & 11
\end{array}
$$

Your students may notice that it is unnecessary to rewrite the sequence of numbers. For example, when 10 is the largest number in the series, the numbers 5 and 11 can calculated as follows:

$$\frac{1}{2} \times 10 = 5$$
$$10 + 1 = 11, \text{ therefore } 5 \times 11 = 55$$

To find the sum of all the whole numbers from 1 to 20 we follow the same process:

$$\frac{1}{2} \times 20 = 10$$
$$20 + 1 = 21, \text{ therefore } 10 \times 21 = 210$$

So $1 + 2 + 3 + \ldots + 20 = 10 \times 21 = 210$.

Similarly,
$$1 + 2 + 3 + \ldots 50 = 25 \times 51 = 1275$$
$$1 + 2 + 3 + \ldots 15 = 7.5 \times 16 = 120$$

Have your class experiment with different series to see if the rule always seems to work.

Problem and Solution 10

CLASS ALLOWANCE
(Problem Starter Sheet 10, page 106)
How much money does your class spend in a year?

Solution: Class Allowance
Understand the Problem
Facts
- Many children in the United States don't realize how much money they spend.

Conditions
- Include only money that children actually spend themselves (not money spent "on" them).

Goal
- Find out how much the whole class spends in a year.

Select a Strategy
Individuals or small groups work out their spending habits for a year. Approximate weekly allowance (income) and spending should be estimated for each student. You might want to discuss different spending habits during the summer and holidays. Savings should be subtracted. Use a calculator to total weekly spending for the whole class and multiply by 52 to find yearly consumer power.

Carry Out the Strategy
Have each student total personal spending for one week. Include milk and lunch money and allowance or earnings spent on school supplies, food, toys, comic books, and so on. Discuss estimation skills to help your class understand what "average spending per week" means.

Once everyone has computed their estimated average weekly spending, organize the results in a table and have the class fill in their own personal record sheets as well. Have each student compute the class weekly spending and multiply by 52 to find their yearly consumer power. Encourage the use of calculators for these computations.

Evaluate the Results
This problem clearly demonstrates the usefulness of gathering statistics in order to investigate an everyday occurrence. Your class (and you) may be surprised at the amount of purchasing power in the 5- to 12-year-old segment of our society. (Saturday morning TV advertisers would not be surprised, however.) The results of this problem can provide the basis for an interesting discussion about spending habits to help children make responsible decisions in the marketplace.

Problem and Solution 11

PENCIL SURVIVAL
(Problem Starter Sheet 11, page 107)
How long does a pencil last in your class? To find out, you will need pencils, tape, and a calculator.

Solution: Pencil Survival
Understand the Problem
Facts
- Pencils are used up at an alarming rate in most classrooms.

Conditions
- It is assumed the pencils sampled are used up at an average rate.

Goal
- Find the average survival rate for a pencil in your class.

Select a Strategy
Label ten new pencils with the date of first use. When the pencil is used up (i.e., too short to sharpen), record the results in a table. After recording the life span of all ten pencils, find the average survival time by dividing the total number of days in use by the number of pencils.

Carry Out the Strategy
The table below shows the life span of ten pencils. Use a calendar to help count the days and compute the average life span. Remember not to count weekends

Date First Sharpened	Date Used Up	Number of School Days Used (Subtract)
1. Sept 15	Sept 19	5
2. Sept 15	Sept 18	4
3. Sept 18	Sept 21	5 *
4. Sept 18	Sept 22	3 *
5. Sept 18	Sept 29	8 *
6. Sept 22	Sept 25	4
7. Sept 22	Sept 30	7 *
8. Sept 22	Sept 23	2
9. Sept 22	Oct 6	11 *
10. Sept 22	Sept 26	5
	Total	**54**

* Don't count weekends

or holidays when the pencils are resting.

To find the average life span, divide the total number of days by the number of pencils: $54 \div 10 = 5.4$ days.

Evaluate the Results
For this sample, the life span of a pencil was a little over five days. If the sample is representative of normal pencil usage, the average life span may be quite accurate. Sampling more pencils over a longer period of time would offer more reliable results, if desired. Try graphing the pencil life span results as below.

Older children can graph the weekly pencil life average to see how their pencil use changes over time.

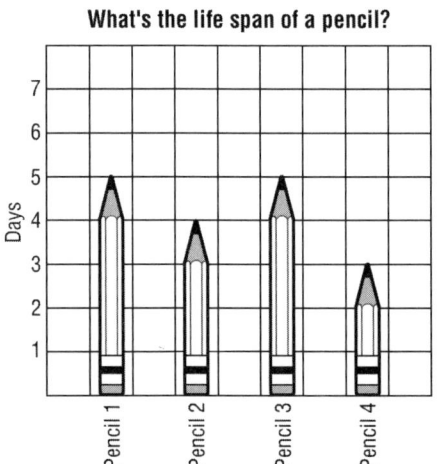
What's the life span of a pencil?

A discussion of how to "read" and interpret graphs would be appropriate at this time. Include terms like *baseline, axis, range,* and *mean (average)*.

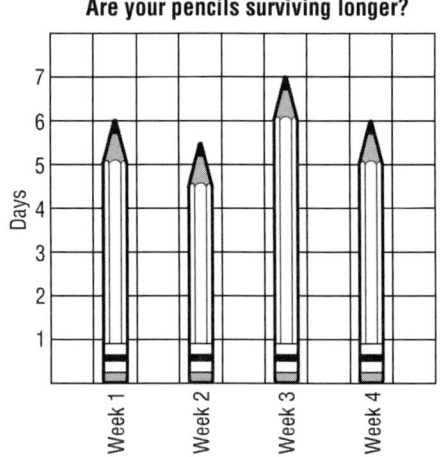
Are your pencils surviving longer?

From *Solving Math Problems Kids Care About*. Copyright © 2006 Good Year Books.

Problem and Solution 12

PAINTING NUMBERS

(Problem Starter Sheet 12, page 108)

A town decided to paint house numbers on the mailbox in front of each home to make it easier for the post office to deliver mail. The houses were numbered in sequence (1, 2, 3, 4, . . .). It cost $1 to paint each digit on the mailboxes. The Town Council determined it needed to budget exactly $600 for the job. How many houses were there in the town?

Solution: Painting Numbers

Understand the Problem

Facts

- Each digit in the house number costs $1.00.
- The house numbers are 1, 2, 3, or possibly more digits long.

Conditions

- The total cost must be exactly $600.
- The house numbers must be sequential (i.e., 1, 2, 3, and so on).
- The addresses must be less than four digits long because if there was even one four-digit house (e.g., 1000), the cost would be more than $600.

Goal

- Find the total number of houses in town.

Select a Strategy

Students should try dividing this problem into subtasks (one-digit, two-digit, and three-digit house numbers) and record the results in a table.

Carry Out the Strategy

First, students should compute the cost of the single-digit house numbers 1 through 9 ($1 × 9 = $9). Next, they can compute the cost for double-digit house numbers 10 through 99 ($2 × 90 = $180), giving a total cost of $189 for the first 99 homes. For the houses numbered 100 through 199, the cost is $300 ($3 × 100 = $300) giving a total cost of $489 for houses 1 through 199. The remaining $111 ($600 − $489 = $111) is enough to paint 37 additional triple-digit numbers (111 ÷ 3 = 37). Organizing the information as in the following table makes the solution of this problem clear.

HOUSE NUMBER PAINTING COST

House Numbers	Cost ($)	Number of Houses
1–9	9	9
10–99	180	90
100–199	300	100
200–236	111	37
Total	**$600**	**236**

Evaluate the Results

The table shows that there must be 236 houses in the town if exactly $600 was budgeted to paint the house numbers. How many houses are there in another city if that other town's council had to budget $2,893 to paint its house numbers?

Problem and Solution 13

T.V. HOURS

(Problem Starter Sheet 13, page 109)
How much television do you watch in one year?

Solution: T.V. Hours

Understand the Problem

Facts
- Families watch varying amounts of television.

Conditions
- The period sampled should be an average week of T.V. viewing.
- The results will depend on how "average" the week is.

Goal
- Determine the number of T.V. viewing hours in one year.

Select a Strategy

Each student should record the number of his or her T.V. viewing hours for one week. Results for one week multiplied by 52 determines the annual T.V. time commitment.

Carry Out the Strategy

The table below is a record of one week's T.V. viewing:

COOPER	T.V. Hours
Monday	3
Tuesday	2
Wednesday	3
Thursday	4
Friday	2
Saturday	6
Sunday	5
Total for Week	**25**
Total for Year (×52)	**1,300**

Evaluate the Results

Cooper watched about 1,300 hours of television in one year. If more or less television viewing took place during the week sampled than throughout the rest of the year, the total viewing hours would of course be inaccurate. However, for our purposes, the estimate is probably accurate enough. If more accurate results are desired, sample two or three randomly chosen

weeks throughout the year and compute the total based on the average of these weekly figures. Some discussion of differing viewing habits during holidays might also be necessary.

It is also fun to compute the total number of hours students are engaged in school, eating, playing, and sleeping. The results can be graphed as shown below, offering a clear picture of life patterns. Each child can construct a personal graph, or an average class graph can be developed to show overall patterns. For younger children, construct the graph showing one week's activities.

What is your life pattern?

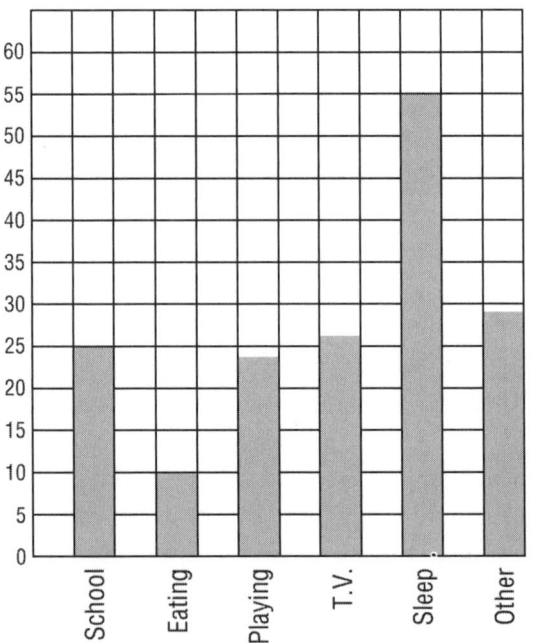

The weekly graph above doesn't tell the whole story, however. Because school is generally in session for 36 weeks, and if we assume that T.V. viewing patterns are consistent throughout the year, this student attended school for only 900 hours and watched 1,300 hours of television—an excellent topic for discussion.

Other topics of interest that can be effectively investigated using graphs include favorite foods, pets, T.V. programs and sports heroes, number of brothers and sisters, and a favorite of ours—a birthday graph! (Also see Tooth Truths, page 32.)

Problem and Solution 14

HOT LUNCH
(Problem Starter Sheet 14, page 110)
Which school lunch does your class like best?

Solution: Hot Lunch
Understand the Problem
Facts
- Some hot lunches are more popular than others.
- Students either bring lunch from home (brownbaggers) or order hot lunch (buyers).

Conditions
- It is assumed that a monthly menu is available to the children ahead of time so free choices can be made.

Goal
- Find out which foods are the most popular.

Select a Strategy
Keep a record of the types of food served each day, the number of buyers and the number of brownbaggers. Using a calculator, compute the percent of students buying lunch for each food item. To compute the percent, simply divide the number of buyers by the total number of students. If an item is served more than once during the month, find the total number of students buying and divide by the total number of students for all the days the item was served. The calculator will show the answer in decimal form. For our purposes we will round to the first two digits. For example:

$$22 \div 32 = 0.6875 = \frac{69}{100} = 69\%$$

Carry Out Plan
The table below shows the lunch-buying habits of a class for one month. Notice that there are 29–32 students in class each day.

MENU

Week	Monday	Tuesday	Wednesday	Thursday	Friday
	Hamburger	Taco	Spaghetti	Pizza	Sloppy Joe
1	Buy 25	Buy 18	Buy 21	Buy 28	Buy 12
	Bring 7	Bring 14	Bring 11	Bring 4	Bring 20
	Total 32	**Total 32**	**Total 32**	**Total 32**	**Total 32**
	Italian Sandwich	Hot Dog	Pizza	Macaroni	Peanut Butter Sand.
2	Buy 23	Buy 15	Buy 29	Buy 5	Buy 25
	Bring 9	Bring 16	Bring 2	Bring 26	Bring 7
	Total 32	**Total 31**	**Total 31**	**Total 31**	**Total 32**
	Sloppy Joe	Hamburger	Spaghetti	Taco	Hot Dog
3	Buy 10	Buy 21	Buy 19	Buy 16	Buy 18
	Bring 22	Bring 9	Bring 10	Bring 15	Bring 12
	Total 32	**Total 30**	**Total 29**	**Total 31**	**Total 30**
	Pizza	Taco	Italian Sandwich	Hamburger	Macaroni
4	Buy 29	Buy 20	Buy 20	Buy 23	Buy 8
	Bring 3	Bring 12	Bring 10	Bring 9	Bring 23
	Total 32	**Total 32**	**Total 30**	**Total 32**	**Total 31**

Organizing the results according to food type, the table below gives a clear picture of food preference.

Type of Food	Total Buyers	Total Students	Percent (Buyers ÷ Total Students)
Hamburger	69	94 (3 days)	73%
Taco	54	95 (3 days)	57%
Spaghetti	40	61 (2 days)	66%
Pizza	86	95 (3 days)	91%
Sloppy Joe	22	64 (2 days)	34%
Italian Sandwich	43	62 (2 days)	69%
Hot Dog	33	61 (2 days)	54%
Macaroni	13	62 (2 days)	21%
Peanut Butter Sandwich	25	32 (1 day)	78%

Graphing the percents in order from small to large helps show the food preferences more clearly.

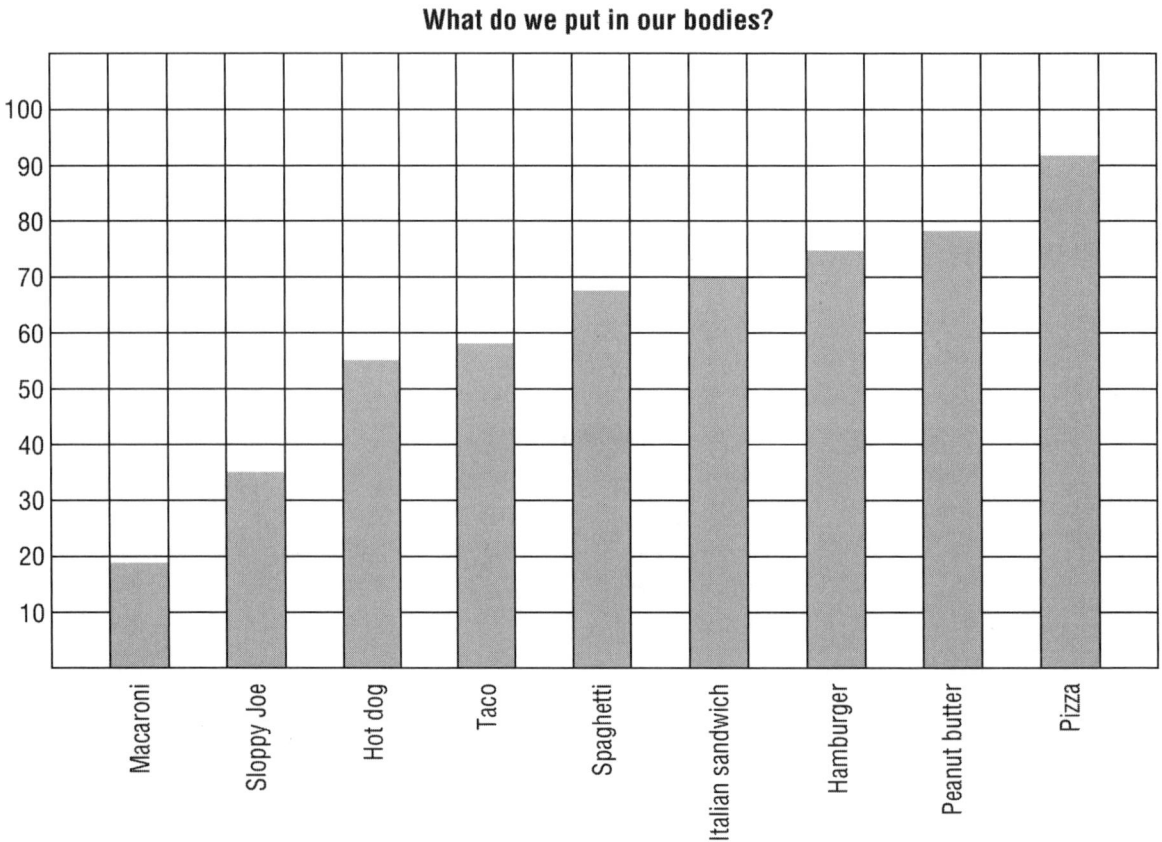

What do we put in our bodies?

Evaluate the Results

Clearly, pizza takes first place in the hot lunch popularity contest. Peanut butter sandwich came in a close second, though we must be careful in interpreting this result, because it was offered only once during the month. Perhaps a late PTA meeting the night before made it difficult for Mom and Dad to pack a lunch at home, so more school lunches would have been bought even if it was liver and onions.

Organizing the percentage graph from least to most gives a clearer picture of the food preferences. Similar graphs can help explain other likes and dislikes. For example, try gathering data on sports and recreational preferences, election predictions, or opinions on school rules. These evaluations can provide students with motivating opportunities to practice analytical skills and strategies for real-world decision-making.

Problem and Solution 15

FOLDING BOXES

(Problem Starter Sheet 15, page 111)

Which of these twelve figures will fold into an open-top box? Fold only on dotted lines.

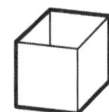

1

2

3

4

5

6

7

8

9

10

11

12

Solution: Folding Boxes

Understand the Problem

Facts

- There are twelve different figures made up of five squares connected to each other along at least one edge.
- Some figures fold into an open-end box.

Conditions

- We must fold along dotted lines only.

Goal

- Determine which figures fold into an open-end box and which do not.

Select a Strategy

Cut out all twelve figures or copy them onto graph paper and cut them out. See which figures fold into an open-end box. Make a list of the results.

Carry Out the Strategy

Of the twelve figures, only 1, 3, 4, 5, 8, 9, and 11 fold into an open-end box. It is impossible to fold the other configurations into a box.

Folds into Open-end Box	Impossible
1, 3, 4, 5, 8, 9, 10, 11	2, 6, 7, 12

Evaluate the Results

This problem can be attacked in two ways. The strategy above works from the given information to the goal (synthesis). We could just as easily cut the tops off several small milk cartons and see which figures can be made by cutting along the edges of each box and laying it flat. Here we are beginning with the goal and working backward to the given figures (analysis). In either case, exactly seven different configurations will be found.

Note: The two figures below are considered to be the same. If we flip one over, it matches exactly with the other.

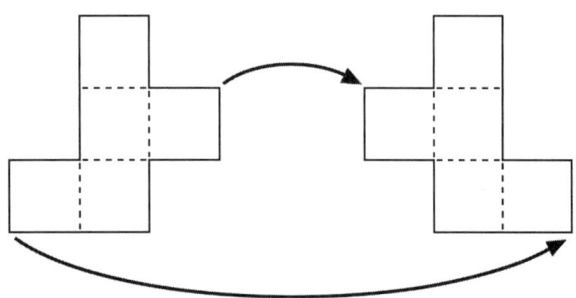

The set of all twelve figures used here are called *pentominoes*. There are a wide range of puzzles and activities that make use of these pieces. For example, if you add one extra 2 x 2 square to give a total of thirteen pieces, it is possible to make an 8 x 8 square using all thirteen pieces with no overlapping

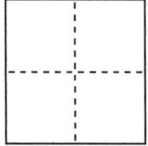

or empty squares. There are many solutions to this puzzle; see if your class can find just one! The following puzzle has been started for you.

Pentomino Puzzle

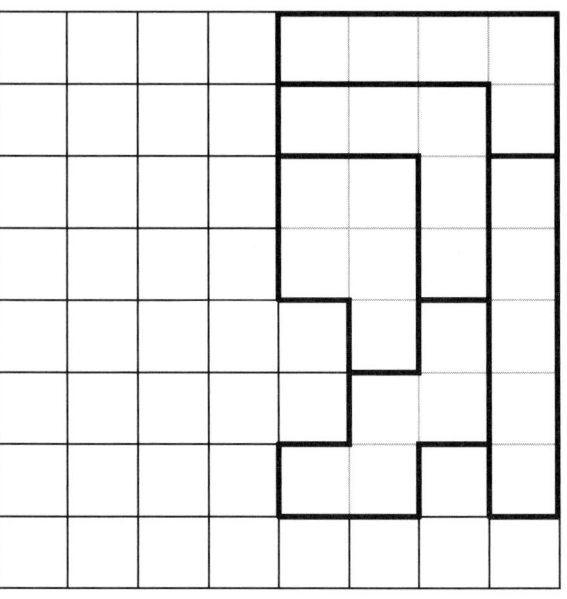

Problem and Solution 16

WHAT'S IN A SHADOW?

(Problem Starter Sheet 16, page 112)
If the shadow of a 6-foot-tall man is 4 feet long, how tall is a tree that casts a 10-foot shadow?

Solution: What's in a Shadow?
Understand the Problem
Facts
- A 10-foot pole casts a shadow twice as long as a 5-foot pole. The heights of the poles are proportional to their shadow lengths.
- A 6-foot object casts a 4-foot shadow.
- The tree's shadow is 10 feet tall.

Conditions
- The shadows of both objects need to be measured at the same time of day.

Goal
- Find the height of the tree.

Select a Strategy
Students can make a scale drawing of the situation using graph paper.

Carry Out the Strategy
Students should label the three known lengths and use a dotted line to represent the unknown tree height. They can then connect the top of the man's head to the end of his shadow to complete the outline of the triangular shadow region. Draw parallel lines connecting each 1-foot marker along the man's shadow to points along the vertical axis representing the man's height. In the figure below, notice that 1 foot of the shadow's length represents 1.5 feet of the man's height.

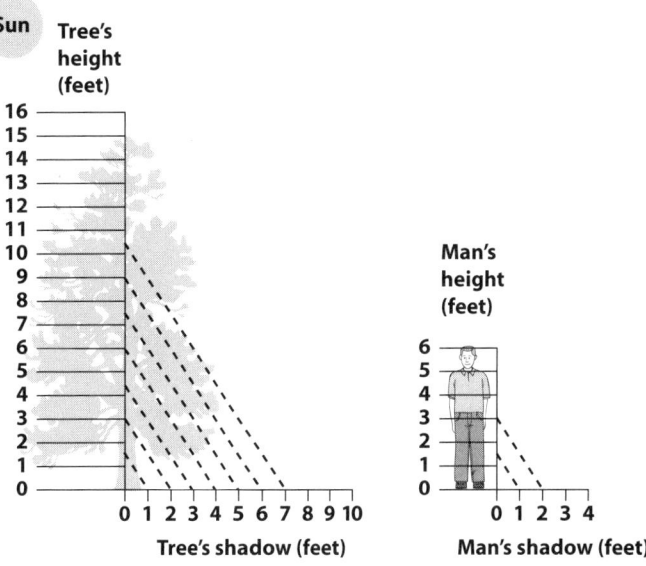

Follow a similar procedure and connect the 1-foot shadow markers the 1.5-foot markers on the vertical lines representing the tree's height. Continue drawing parallel lines until you reach the 10-foot marker on the tree shadow axis. This line crosses the tree height axis at 15 feet.

Evaluate the Results
The tree's height is 15 feet. Every foot of shadow at this particular time of day represents 1.5 feet of the object's height. This relationship can be stated as the ratio of 1.5-to-1. The relationship between object height and shadow length can also be expressed as equivalent ratios using only whole numbers. Notice that the ratios 6 to 4, 3 to 2, and 1.5 to 1 are all equivalent, because ratios can be written as the equivalent fractions 6/4, 3/2, and 2.5/1. An easier way to measure the height of tall objects is to wait until the man's shadow equals his height. At this moment, the height of all objects in the immediate area should equal their shadow lengths (have a ratio of 1 to 1). This would happen at mid-morning or mid-afternoon.

Problem and Solution 17

WHAT'S THE DIFFERENCE?

(Problem Starter Sheet 17, page 113)

Pick any four numbers and write them in a square, as below.

4   8

7   1

Next, connect any two numbers without going across the middle. Find the difference between the two number values and write it at the center of the line.

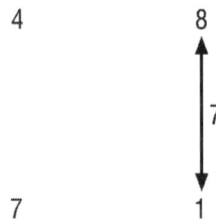

Do the same with the other pairs.

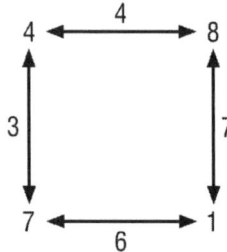

Now connect these numbers with lines and find their differences.

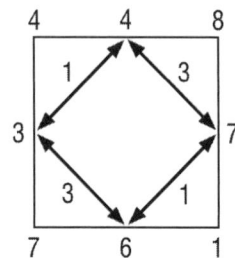

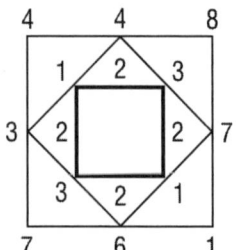

This time all the answers are the same.

Will this always happen for any four starting numbers?

Will you always end up with 2 for a final answer?

What happens if you start with bigger numbers?

This problem needed three steps to get to a common difference. Can you find four numbers that need four steps? Five steps? Six steps?

Solution: What's the Difference?

Understand the Problem

Facts

- Four numbers are placed on the corners of a square.
- Differences are found for each pair of adjacent numbers.
- These four answers are again connected in a square array and the difference found as before. The process is continued until you arrive at a common answer.

Conditions

- Always compute the positive difference between two numbers. For example, the difference between 3 and 5 is 2, not –2.

Goal

- Find out if you always end at a common difference for any four numbers. Does this final answer vary? Can you find four numbers that require four steps to arrive at a common difference? Five steps? Six steps? Seven steps?

Select a Strategy

Try many combinations of four numbers. Record the original numbers and the numbers of steps it takes you to reach a common difference and the final answer.

Carry Out a Strategy

The table below lists the results of several experiments:

LEAH'S RECORD SOLUTION

4 Numbers	Number of Steps	Common Difference
4, 8, 1, 7	3	2
3, 88, 99, 57	3	27
1, 2, 8, 4	5	2
1, 2, 4, 8	6	2
1, 3, 9, 27	5	8
12, 77, 2, 25	3	42
2, 5, 7, 1	4	2
3, 6, 9, 12	1	3
15, 8, 11, 4	2	4
15, 3, 4, 8	7	4

Evaluate the Results

Every example seems to arrive eventually at a common difference. The final answer varies and the number of steps ranges from one to six. We have been unable to find an example that requires more than seven steps to arrive at a common difference. Perhaps your class can find a set of four numbers that requires more than seven steps.

An interesting extension of this problem involves rearranging the order of a set of numbers and observing the required number of differences to arrive at a common answer. [See (1, 2, 8, 4) and (1, 2, 4, 8) above.] The final difference seems to be the same but the number of steps varies. Is this the case for other sets of numbers? A calculator may help with this one.

Problem and Solution 18

GOLD DIGGERS

(Problem Starter Sheet 18, page 114)
Digger Jenkins was a gold assayer who flew all over Alaska in a rickety little plane weighing ore for eager prospectors. His job was to weigh samples very accurately, but he also had to be careful not to overload his tiny plane with equipment. To measure weight, he packed only three mass pieces—1-gram, 3-gram, and 9-gram weights. For example, he could weigh a 4-gram sample of gold ore like this:

4-gram ore sample   1-gram & 3-gram weights

Digger claimed he could weigh any amount of ore from 1 to 13 grams. (No fractions, of course.) Is Digger right?

Solution: Gold Diggers
Understand the Problem
Facts
- You must use a pan balance and three mass pieces—1, 3, and 9 grams.
- You can put one or more pieces of mass on either pan.

Conditions
- You can only weigh to the nearest whole gram.

Goal
- How many different weights can be measured using only 1-, 3- and 9-gram mass pieces?

Select a Strategy
Using a pan balance and three mass pieces, weigh out several piles of sand or rice. Record the results in a table.

Carry Out a Strategy
Conduct a few experiments with the pan balance.

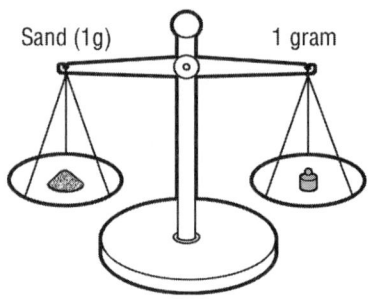

Sand (1g)   1 gram

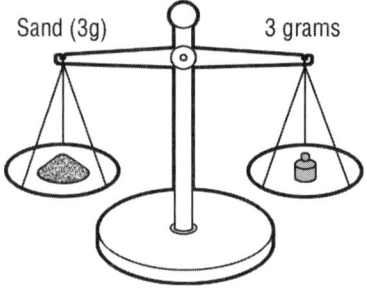

Sand (3g)   3 grams

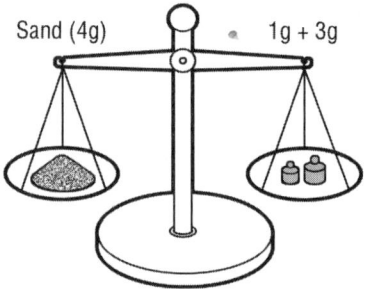

Sand (4g)   1g + 3g

The key to weighing 2 and 5 grams of sand is to realize that by placing mass pieces on both pans, you actually subtract (counterbalance) the mass of the small weight from the larger. It may be possible for some children to complete the table without actually carrying out all the weighings.

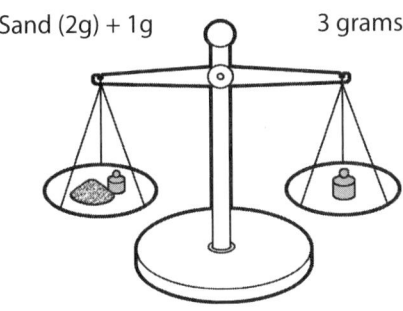

Sand (2g) + 1g   3 grams

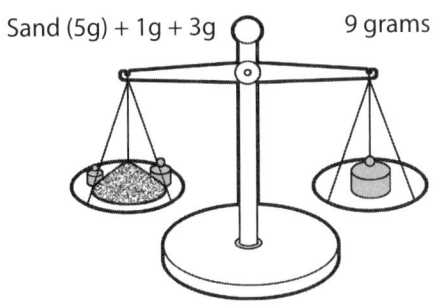

Sand (5g) + 1g + 3g   9 grams

Evaluate the Results

It is in fact possible for Digger to weigh piles of ore from 1 to 13 grams in mass. It is rather remarkable that these three mass pieces allow such a large number of weighings. These pieces were chosen because of this unique property of base 3. You might find it interesting to see how many weighings are possible when four mass pieces are used—1 gram, 3 grams, 9 grams, and 27 grams. The results are quite surprising. Base-2 mass pieces (1, 2, 4, 8, 16, 32, etc.) offer similar weighing properties, though more mass pieces are needed. Base-2 mass pieces have the added advantage of requiring placement only on the right hand pan. Try other bases (4, 5, 10) to see which requires the fewest mass pieces to measure any whole-number mass.

MASS OF SAND

(GRAMS)	LEFT PAN	RIGHT PAN
1	sand	1 gram
2	sand + 1 gram m.p.	3 gram m.p
3	sand	3 gram m.p.
4	sand	1 gram m.p. + 3 gram m.p.
5	sand + 1 gram m.p. + 3 gram m.p.	9 gram m.p.
6	sand + 3 gram m.p.	9 gram m.p.
7	sand + 3 gram m.p.	1 gram m.p. + 9 gram m.p.
8	sand + 1 gram m.p.	9 gram m.p.
9	sand	9 gram m.p.
10	sand	1 gram m.p. + 9 gram m.p.
11	sand + 1 gram m.p.	3 gram + 9 gram m.p.
12	sand	3 gram m.p. + 9 gram m.p.
13	sand	1 gram m.p. + 3 gram m.p + 9 gram m.p.

(m.p. = mass piece)

THE GREAT DIVIDE

(Problem Starter Sheet 19, page 115)

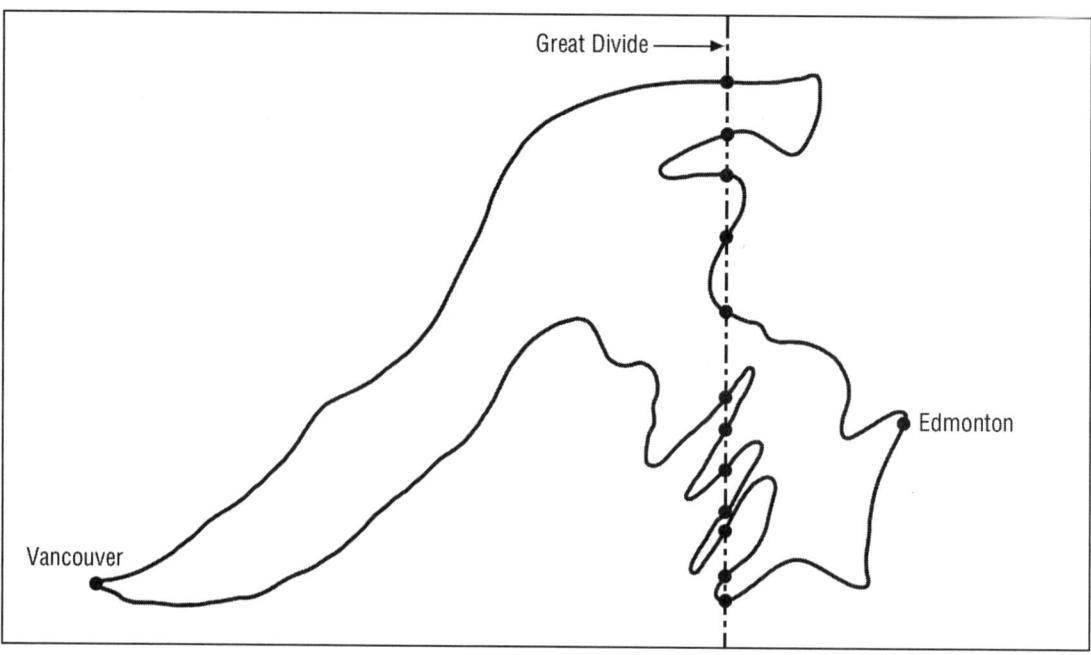

Otto Levique and his family were taking a trip across Canada by car. When they came to the Rocky Mountains, his daughter, Michelle, who had been studying geography in school, explained that they would soon cross the Great Divide—an imaginary line running lengthwise along the highest points of a mountain range. Rain falling to the east of this line ends up in the Atlantic Ocean; rain to the west ends up in the Pacific Ocean. It was an exciting moment, when they crossed the "roof of the continent," but they were all surprised when they crossed the imaginary line more than once. Look at the map to see how this could happen.

Michelle kept a record of the number of times they crossed the Great Divide. She thought it was odd that they crossed the line five times on their route from Edmonton to Vancouver and seven times on their return, making a total of twelve crossings for the round trip. Will every round trip through the mountains always have an even number of Great Divide crossings? Help the Leviques with the auto-dilemma.

Solution: The Great Divide
Understand the Problem
Facts
- The Great Divide is an imaginary line connecting the highest points, lengthwise, along a mountain range.
- The road weaves back and forth across the line as it works its way through the mountains.

Conditions
- You must make a round trip from Edmonton to Vancouver to Edmonton.
- You cannot go around mountains, through the Panama Canal, or across the Arctic.

Goal
- Find out if you must always cross the Great Divide an even number of times when making a round trip.

Select a Strategy

Draw a map and conduct several experiments. Organize the data in a table and look for patterns.

Carry Out a Strategy

The following maps show several configurations of routes and Great Divides. The results of these two routes along with others are summarized in the table that follows.

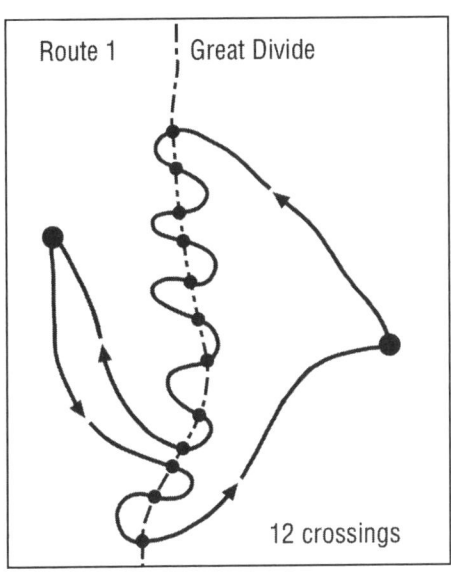

12 crossings

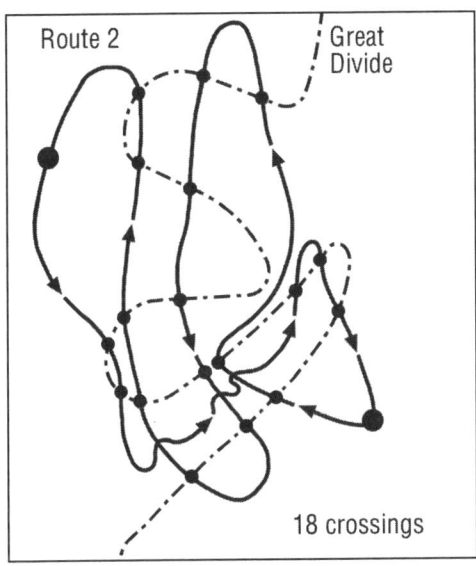

18 crossings

ROUTE	NUMBER OF CROSSINGS		
	Going	Returning	Total
1	9	3	12
2	13	5	18
3	1	1	2
4	3	1	4
5			
6			

Evaluate the Results

A clear pattern emerges. No matter how convoluted the path of the Great Divide, any route through the range in one direction will cross an odd number of times. (The Great Divide cannot cross itself, however.) A round trip requires an odd-plus-odd (even) number of crossings. You and your students may want to justify to yourselves that the sum of two odd numbers is, in fact, always even.

Though discovering a pattern doesn't guarantee that it will work for all cases, at the elementary level deductive proofs (which do offer such guarantees) may not be appropriate. If everyone in the class does several experiments and the pattern holds, this "proof by desire" seems sufficient.

As an alternative solution, it is interesting to note that because you can not make an "end run" around the Great Divide line, the situation is identical to counting the number of times you go through your front door each day from when you get out of bed until you return at night. There is a tradition in rural New England that says that the greatest comfort in life is living in the house you were born in. The only way in which you can sit in any house having the comfort of knowing that you have passed through the door an even number of times is to have been born there. Everyone else having dinner with you will have passed through an odd number of times.

Problem and Solution 20

MAKING A RACE FAIR

(Problem Starter Sheet 20, page 116)
A turtle and a rabbit ran a 1,000-meter race. The turtle ran 10 meters each minute and the rabbit ran 100 meters each minute. The turtle was also given a 500-meter head start. Who won the race? Was it a fair race?

Solution: Make a Race Fair

Understand the Problem

Facts

- The turtle started the race at the 500-meter mark.
- The rabbit started at the 0-meter mark

Conditions

- Let's assume the turtle ran a constant 10 meters per minute and the rabbit ran 100 meters per minute.
- The turtle either reached the finish line first or the rabbit passed the turtle somewhere between the 500-meter mark and the finish line.

Goal

- Who won the race and was the race fair?

Select a Strategy

Have students construct a graph that shows the progress of the turtle and rabbit from beginning of the race to the end.

Carry Out the Strategy

Ask students to plot the racetrack distance along the vertical axis and the race time along the horizontal axis as shown in the figure. The rabbit started at the 0 mark and ran 100 meters each minute. They can follow the rabbit's progress by plotting a point that represents the time it takes to cover each 100 meters (point A represents 1 minute for 100 meters; point B represents 2 minutes for 200 meters; and so on). Connecting these points with a line gives a graph of the rabbit's speed. A similar procedure is followed for the turtle that started at the 500-meter mark. Due to his slower pace, the graph of the turtle's speed is not as steep as the graph of the rabbit.

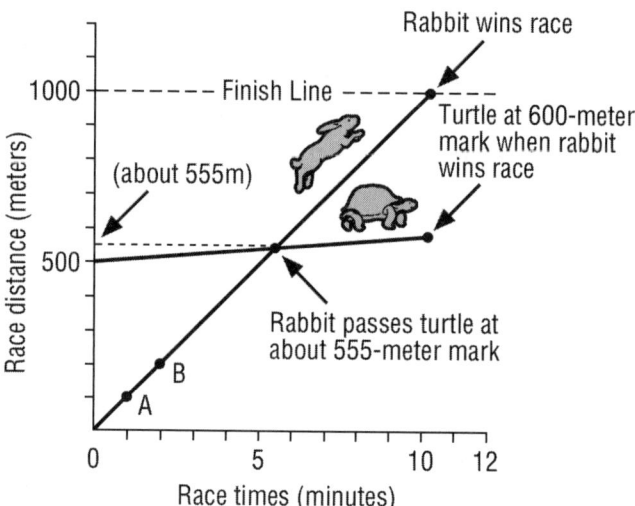

Evaluate the Results

The rabbit won the race. The graph shows that the rabbit passed the turtle at about the 555-meter mark. The turtle was at the 600-meter mark when the rabbit crossed the finish line. The race took ten minutes. If the turtle continued the race, it would finish forty minutes after the rabbit, which can also be shown on the graph. Based on the expected performance of both contestants, the race was not fair. The turtle would need to start at the 900-meter mark to have a sporting chance to win. This process is called *handicapping* and is used in golf, horse racing, and other sports. Handicapping allows players with differing levels of skill to compete in the same game, giving everyone the same chance to win.

Problem and Solution 21

STACK THE DECK

(Problem Starter Sheet 21, page 117)
Here is an interesting card trick to try with your friends. Write each letter of your name on separate, identical cards. Form them into a deck with the faces down and shuffle the deck. Slip the top card under the deck, still facedown. Deal the second card faceup on the table. Slip the third card under the deck and deal the next card faceup next to the first. Continue this process until all the cards form a line on the table.

You would be lucky indeed if the cards spelled a word. However, can you find a way to stack the deck so that when you deal out the cards as above, it spells your name?

If you can figure out a solution, it's fun to surprise your friends by using their names.

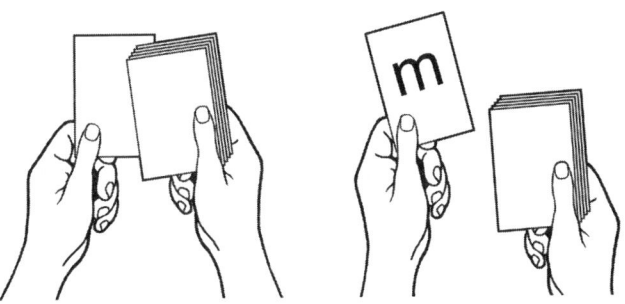

Slip one card under deck. Deal next card faceup.

Solution: Stack the Deck
Understand the Problem
Facts
- Each letter of a name is written on separate, identical cards.
- The cards are dealt one at a time. You slip the first card under the deck, place the second card faceup on the table, slip the third card under the deck, place the next card faceup, and so on.
- Stop when all cards are on the table.

Conditions
- Cards should be placed next to each other on the table from left to right. *Note:* It is possible to spell out the names backward to heighten the element of surprise.

Goal
- Arrange the deck so that when it is dealt out in the above manner, the cards will spell out a name.

Select a Strategy
Have students try working the problem backward by first spelling out the name on the table, then reversing the dealing procedure until they have a completed deck. If their name is long, they can try a shorter one for practice. Initially, it might be helpful to use numbered playing cards instead of letters. They can use the same strategy, but begin with a series of cards numbered from 1 to 10.

Carry Out a Strategy
Begin with the cards arranged on the table as in the example below.

Pick up the last card (E) and place it facedown on top of the deck. (The deck has zero cards at the beginning.) Slip the bottom card on the top, facedown. (The bottom card is the top card in this case, so nothing changes.) Place the next card (I) on top (facedown) and slip the bottom card (E) facedown on top. Continue this process until all the cards are in the deck. When finished, the deck should be in the following order (top to bottom).

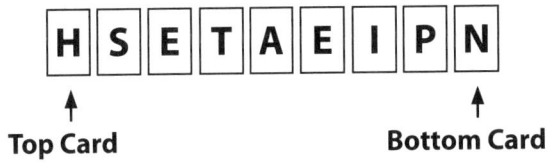

If you use a series of numbered cards (1 to 10), begin as below and follow the same procedure.

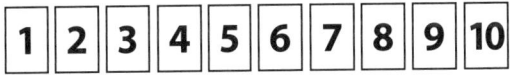

The order of the deck should be (top to bottom): 8, 1, 6, 2, 10, 3, 7, 4, 9, 5

Evaluate the Results

Reverse the process and the deck should "spell" the name or number sequence correctly. Any sequence of letters or numbers can be arranged into a deck in this manner.

It is interesting to compare this problem to "Clyde the Class Clown" (Problem Solution Sheet 38). If you simply arrange the deck of number cards from 1 to 10 (1 on top and 10 on bottom) and deal them out as described above, the last card will tell you the "lucky" position for a class of ten.

Some additional problems that might challenge your class include arranging the deck to:

1. Spell their first and last names.
2. Spell their names backward.
3. Count down from 10 to 1.
4. Write a friend's telephone number.
5. Spell out a funny saying.
6. Spell out a secret message.
7. Spell out their names but slip two cards under the deck each time instead of one.

Problem and Solution 22

FOUR ACES

(Problem Starter Sheet 22, page 118)
This simple card trick sounds complicated but it is actually very easy to do.

1. Using an ordinary deck of cards, cut the cards into four roughly equal piles and lay them out next to each other in front of you.
2. Pick up the pile that came from the bottom of the deck (pile 4), and deal three cards facedown on the table in the same spot where the pile was.
3. Deal one card from pile 4 facedown on top of each of the other three decks and place the pile back where it came from, on top of the three cards.
4. Repeat the process with the other three piles, ending with the pile that was on top of the original deck (pile 1).
5. Turning over the top card on each pile gives a surprising result—four aces!

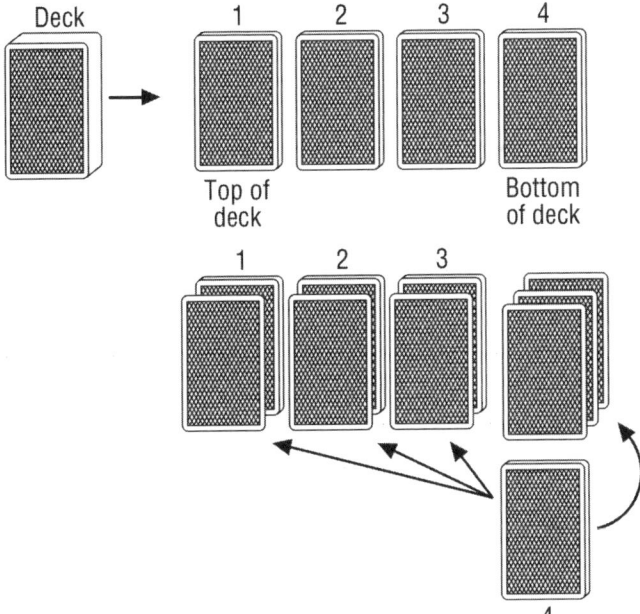

- Pick up pile 4
- Deal 3 cards facedown
- Deal 1 card on piles 1, 2, and 3
- Replace pile 4
- Repeat process with 1, 2, and 3

Can you figure out how the trick works?

Solution: Four Aces
Understand the Problem
Facts
- You use a regular deck of cards.
- Cut the deck into four piles with the top pile on the left (pile 1) and bottom pile on the right (pile 4). Pick up the bottom pile (4), deal three cards down in same spot where pile 4 was, then deal one card facedown on each of the other piles. Repeat with other piles, ending with pile 1.

Conditions
- Cards in the original deck must be prearranged to exorcise the "magic."

Goal
- Find out how the original deck was arranged in order to explain the "magic."

Select a Strategy
Students should work the problem backward, keeping track of the four aces to see how to stack the original deck.

Carry Out the Strategy
Starting with the final result, reverse each step in the process.

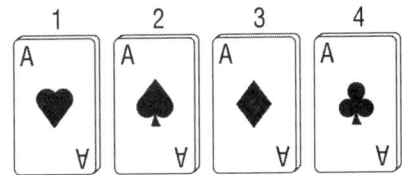

1. Turn the aces facedown on top of the four piles.

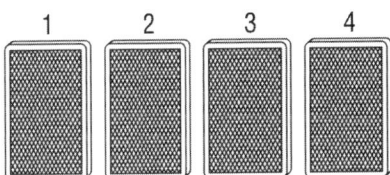

2. Pick up the top card on each pile and put them on top of pile 1.

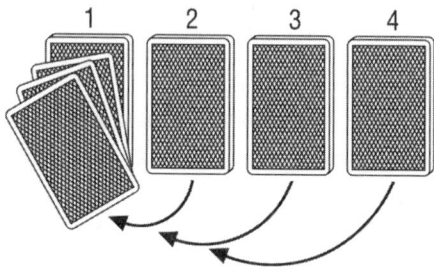

Note: The four aces are now on top of pile 1.

3. Pick up pile 1. Put the bottom three cards on top of the pile.

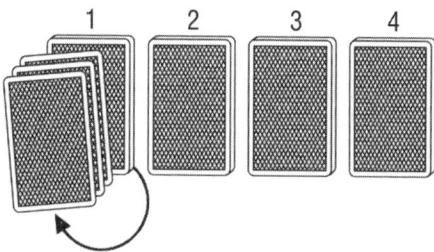

Note: The aces in pile 1 are now under three cards.

4. Pick up pile 2. Place one card from the top of piles 1, 3, and 4 on pile 2. Move the bottom three cards to top of pile 2 and replace the pile in its original position. Aces still in pile 1 are now under two cards.
5. Repeat this process two more times using piles 3 and 4. Aces in pile 1 are now on top of the pile.
6. Pick up the four piles in order with 1 on the top and 4 on the bottom.

Evaluate the Results
To set up the deck for the trick, simply place four aces on top of the deck. The rest of the trick works automatically. All of the moving around of cards and piles is simply to confuse the observers. Like most card tricks, if your audience knew how simple it was, they would be quite upset with themselves.

As you may have noticed, you can change the order in which the piles are picked up, except pile1 must be used last. Many card tricks of this type can be invented by your students, offering an excellent opportunity for them to develop their organizational skills and short-term memory.

From *Solving Math Problems Kids Care About.* Copyright © 2006 Good Year Books.

Problems and Solutions 23

STACK 'EM HIGH

(Problem Starter Sheet 23, page 119)
Suzanne Megapenny is very rich. She got a bit bored one day and told her banker to immediately deliver one million new one-dollar bills to her house. She sat in her living room and began to stack the bills on top of each other in a single column. How high will the stack be?

Solution: Stack 'Em High

Understanding the Problem

Facts

- Megapenny has one million new one-dollar bills.
- She is making a single stack of bills, each bill on top of the other.

Conditions

- Assume a dollar bill is about the same thickness as a book page.
- Because the bills are new, you don't need to consider wrinkles.

Goal

- Estimate the height of the stack of one million one-dollar bills.

Select a Strategy

Have students estimate the number of dollar bills in a stick 1-centimeter thick by measuring a 1-centimeter thickness on the edge of a book and counting the pages. They can divide one million by the number of pages in 1 centimeter to find out how many centimeter thicknesses would be required.

Carry Out the Strategy

Students should measure a 1-centimeter thickness across the end of a book. They can count the pages to find out the approximate number of dollars in a 1-cm-thick stack. A short cut to counting is to open any book to page 1 and measure a depth of 1 cm. Dividing the last page number in the stack by 2 gives you the total number of pages. Can your class figure out why?

Let's say there are 80 pages per centimeter. Dividing 1,000,000 by 80 gives the number of centimeter stacks needed. For example, if I had 250 one-dollar bills, the height of the stack would equal 250 ÷ 80, or approximately 3 cm. Therefore, one million dollars would stack up:

$$1,000,000 \div 80 = 125,000 \text{ cm or } 125 \text{ meters high!}$$

Evaluate the Results

To get an idea of how tall this is, remember that a room is about 3 meters high. Megapenny's living room would have to be more than 42 stories high to hold all that wealth.

From Solving Math Problems Kids Care About. Copyright © 2006 Good Year Books.

Problem and Solution 24

COUNT ON

(Problem Starter Sheet 24, page 120)

One rainy afternoon Tara couldn't find anyone to play with so she decided to count to a billion. Can you find out about how long it would take Tara to finish? One hour? Two hours? All day? How old are you in seconds?

Solution: Count on

Understanding the Problem

Facts

- Use natural numbers (1, 2, 3, 4, 5, . . .).

Conditions

- Count steady at a rate of one number a second.

Goal

- Find out how long it will take Tara to count to one billion.

Select a Strategy

For simplicity, have students estimate that it takes one second to count each number. Using a calculator, ask them to figure out how high Tara could count in an hour, a day, a week, and a year. Organize the results in a table.

Carry Out the Strategy

The following table lists how high you could count in a second, minute, hour, day, and so on, if you count one number each second.

Time	Count
1 second	1
1 minute	60
1 hour	3600
1 day	86,400
1 week	604,800
1 year	31,449,600
10 years	314,496,000 *
30 years	943,488,000 (Almost there.)
32 years	1,006,387,200 (We made it!)

*Most calculators give up here and overflow.

Evaluate the Results

This problem clearly demonstrates the limitations of the simple handheld calculator. The largest number most calculators can show accurately is 99,999,999, far smaller than our goal. In fact, we can calculate only a little more than three years' worth of counting. A bit of "old-fashioned" arithmetic quickly shows that Tara would have to count day and night for more than thirty-one years to reach her goal. It would certainly be a long rainy afternoon.

Using the table, it is easy to figure your age in seconds. Anyone older than three years will have to figure it out by hand, however, unless they have a very fancy calculator. As of October 3, 2005, the author was exactly 1,510,330,800 seconds old. Can you figure out his birthday and age?

Problems and Solutions 25

GRAINS OF RICE

(Problem Starter Sheet 25, page 121)
How many grains of rice are in a bag of rice? One hundred grains? One thousand grains? One million grains? To find out you need a bag of rice, a pan-balance scale, and a calculator.

Solution: Grains of Rice
Understand the Problem
Facts
- A bag of rice contains many grains.
- The grains are about the same size.
- Two common sizes are 1-kilogram and 1-pound bags.

Conditions
- You have access to only a pan balance, small cups, and a calculator.

Goal
- Find the approximate number of grains in a bag of rice.

Select a Strategy
Have students follow these steps: Measure out one small cup of rice. Any small coffee-creamer-sized cups will work. Count the grains. For younger children, a team approach to this counting task may be in order. Using the balance, weigh out quantities of rice one cup at a time to find the total number of cups in a bag. This process can be speeded up considerably by first measuring out one cup on each side of the balance. Next, place both measured cups on the same pan and pour rice on the other pan until it balances. Again put the two piles together on one pan (now four cups) and weigh out an equivalent amount on the balance. Continuing this process of doubling (1, 2, 8, 16, . . . cups), one is able to quickly determine the number of cups in the bag. Using a calculator, multiply the number of grains in one cup by the total number of cups to find the total number of grains in the bag.

Carry Out the Strategy
The number of grains in a coffee-creamer cup is about 1,135. A kilogram bag of rice contains approximately 38 creamer-cups of rice. The total number of grains is $38 \times 1{,}135 = 43{,}130$ grains.

Evaluate the Results
The answer above is only approximate. Its accuracy depends on the consistency in grain size and accuracy in measurement. Obviously there will be errors; however, the answer does give a reasonable approximation to the number of grains.

The size of the measuring cup isn't important, though a small one simplifies the counting process and minimizes error due to a fractional part of a cup left over when weighing out the whole bag.

An interesting extension to this problem for older children is to consider how large a packing crate would be required to contain one million grains of rice. You might even want to set your class to work finding the number of grains of rice it would take to fill your classroom. Would a billion grains do it? How many grains of rice are in one serving? How many people would it take to eat a room full of rice?

Problem and Solution 26

MONEY MATTERS

(Problem Starter Sheet 26, page 122)

One day, Rosa decided to play a trick on her brother, Aaron. She said, "I have 21¢ in my pocket. If you can tell me all the possible combinations of pennies, nickels, and dimes that make up 21¢, I'll buy you an ice cream cone." Here is one way:

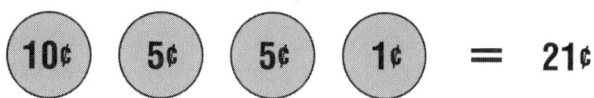

After Aaron started making his list, Rosa said, "I just found a dollar in my other pocket. If you can find all the ways to make change for $1.21, I'll buy you a double-dipper cone. You can use pennies, nickels, dimes, quarters, half dollars, and a silver dollar." Here is one way:

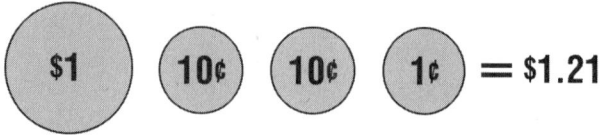

Can you help Aaron find all the ways to make change for 21¢? For $1.21?

Solution: Money Matters

Understand the Problem

Facts

- First Rosa had 21¢ in her pocket, then she had $1.21 in her pocket.
- You can use 1¢, 5¢, 10¢, 25¢, 50¢, and $1 coins.

Conditions

- You can use as many coins as necessary.
- You are not required to use all six coins at once.

Goal

- List all possible combinations of coins equaling 21¢ and $1.21.

Select a Strategy

Students can construct a list of combinations of one or more coins that equal 21¢. They can begin with the largest possible coin and list all possible combinations with smaller coins. Then they can systematically reduce the size of the initial coin until they reach 21 pennies. Try the same task for $1.21.

Carry Out the Strategy

The table below lists all the combinations of pennies, nickels, and dimes adding up to 21¢. The key to the solution is being systematic in listing the combinations so you will know when you are finished.

	Change for 21¢		
	10¢	5¢	1¢
1	2	0	1
2	1	2	1
3	1	1	6
4	1	0	11
5	0	4	1
6	0	3	6
7	0	2	11
8	0	1	16
9	0	0	21

Evaluate the Results

There are exactly nine ways to make change for 21¢. Aaron should have no problem collecting his first scoop of ice cream. Trying a similar procedure for $1.21, however, presents a surprisingly complex situation. We now have to keep track of six types of coins (pennies, nickels, dimes, quarters, half dollars, and dollars). The number of combinations grows distressingly fast, trying the patience of even the most loving brother. If you or your students try to solve this one, you can at least have satisfaction in knowing that the author stayed up late into the night completing the table. Aaron would have to work hard indeed for that double dipper, because there are 782 ways to make change for $1.21!

Problem and Solution 27

ICE-CREAM EXPERT

(Problem Starter Sheet 27, page 123)
Bud was an expert ice-cream eater. He could name any flavor blindfolded. When he bought an ice cream cone, not only did he choose the flavors carefully, but he had to have them stacked on the cone in the right order. Strawberry on top with vanilla on the bottom was for hot days. Vanilla on top and strawberry on the bottom helped him to think better.

There are only two ways of building a cone with two flavors. (You must use both flavors.) How many different cones could Bud order with three flavors? Four flavors? Five flavors?

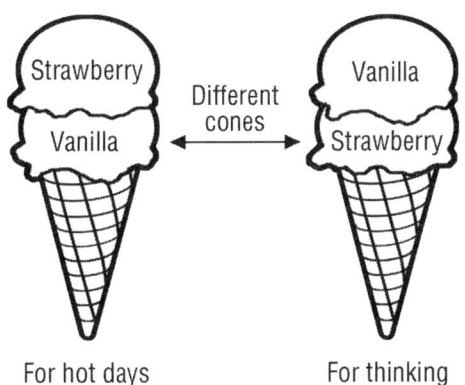

For hot days   For thinking

Solution: Ice-Cream Expert
Understand the Problem
Facts
- Ice-cream scoops stack one on top of the other.
- Ice-cream scoops stacked in various order are considered different.

Conditions
- You must use all the chosen flavors on each cone.

Goal
- Find the number of different cones that can be made from three, four, and five flavors.

Select a Strategy
Students can develop a table of different cones starting with one flavor, then two, and so on. They can construct the list in a systematic manner to ensure that no possibilities are skipped. They can then count the total number of cones (called *permutations*) and try to discover a pattern involving the number of flavors and the number of cones.

Carry Out the Strategy
The table below lists all the permutations of scoops for one through four flavors.

Number of different cones
(Must use all flavors)

S – Strawberry   C – Chocolate
V – Vanilla   P – Pecan

Flavors	Combinations	Total cones
1		1
2		2
3		6
4		24

Evaluate the Results
Notice that list is "growing" very quickly. Many times when solving a problem, it is useful to look for a pattern in order to reduce the amount of labor. Some problems get so complicated that you must find an arithmetical shortcut in order to finish in a reasonable amount of time. Such is the case with the current problem. Observe the following table:

Number of Flavors	Number of Cones
1	1
2	2
3	6
4	24
5	?

Notice that to find the number of permutations of, say, three flavors, simply multiply 3 by the number of cones for two flavors:

$$3 \times 2 = 6$$

Does this pattern always hold?

$$2 \times 1 = 2$$
$$3 \times 2 = 6$$
$$4 \times 6 = 24$$
$$5 \times 24 = 120$$

Notice that if the pattern holds, the number of possible cones using five flavors is 120! Consider how permutations grow by adding an additional flavor, you are simply taking the previous set of cones (say, six cones for three flavors) and giving each of the four flavors a chance to be on top ($4 \times 6 = 24$). The table can be continued as below:

Number of Flavors	Number of Cones
1	1
2	2
3	6
4	24
5	120
6	720
7	5,040
8	40,320

It is interesting to note that this pattern actually describes the process of multiplying together all the natural numbers up to and including the number of flavors considered. For example, with five flavors there are:

$$1 \times 2 \times 3 \times 4 \times 5 = 120 \text{ cones}$$

Mathematicians call this process *calculating the factorial*. We use the notation below to indicate the factorial calculation.

$$5! = 120$$

It should be easy to determine the number of permutations for various numbers of flavors. Have your students find out the largest factorial their calculator can swallow.

Problem and Solution 28

WHO'S SHAKING WHOSE

(Problem Starter Sheet 28, page 124)
If ten people are attending a meeting, how many handshakes are required for each person to greet every other person exactly once?

Solution: Who's Shaking Whose
Understand the Problem
Facts
- There are ten people at the meeting.

Conditions
- It takes two people to shake hands.
- If person 1 shakes hands with person 2, it is the same as person 2 shaking hands with person 1.

Goal
- How many total handshakes are necessary for each person to shake hands exactly once with every other person at the meeting.

Select a Strategy
Students can construct a table that lists the number of handshakes required for each person if one person initiates the greeting at a time.

Carry Out the Strategy
The first person must shake hands with nine people. Once these greetings are accomplished, person 1 can sit down at the conference table. The next person then shakes hands with the eight remaining persons. The following table shows the results of this process.

Evaluate the Results
The table shows that a total of forty-five handshakes are required for ten persons to greet each other exactly once. A similar table can be constructed for handshakes at larger meetings—for example, for 20 people ($19 + 18 + 17 + \ldots + 1 + 0 = 190$), 100 people ($99 + 98 + 97 + \ldots + 1 + 0 = 4950$) or 1,000 people ($999 + 998 + 997 + \ldots + 1 + 0 = 499{,}500$). Have students try to work out the formula that will calculate the number of handshakes (h) based on the number of people (p) at the meetings.

$$[(p - 1) \times (\tfrac{p}{2})] = h$$

Students might also enjoy figuring out how to calculate the number of handshakes needed at a meeting if the custom was changed so that three persons shook hands at one time instead of two.

Handshakes

Person #	1	2	3	4	5	6	7	8	9	10
# of Handshakes	9 +	8 +	7 +	6 +	5 +	4 +	3 +	2 +	1 +	0 = 45

Problem and Solution 29

HAMBURGER HEAVEN

(Problem Starter Sheet 29, page 125)

HAMBURGER HEAVEN

Burgers		Fries 'n' Rings		Drinks	
1. Boring Burger.......	30¢	1. French Fries	45¢	1. Orange..................	38¢
2. Kiloburger.............	75¢	2. Onion Rings	65¢	2. Cola.......................	30¢
3. Fat Burger.........	$1.50			3. Root Beer............	30¢
				4. Milk........................	55¢

If you are allowed to pick one item from each column, how many different meals could you make? Here are two different meals:

1. Fat Burger, Onion Rings, Root Beer
2. Fat Burger, French Fries, Milk

How many meals would be possible if one more type of hamburger was added to the menu?

Solution: Hamburger Heaven

Understand the Problem

Facts

- There are three types of hamburgers, two types of fries, and four types of drinks.

Conditions

- Must choose one item from each column to be called a meal.
- A meal is "different" if one item changed.

Goal

- Find out how many different meals can be constructed from Hamburger Heaven's menu.

Select a Strategy

Students can develop a list of possible meals using a systematic process so no combination will be overlooked. Abbreviating the food names might simplify the listing process.

Carry Out the Strategy

The following list was formed by selecting the first item in each row. We then changed only the drink, giving us the first four meals. Next we changed the french fries (FF) to onion rings (OR) and repeated the process, giving four more meals. We then changed to the second burger and repeated from the start, giving eight more meals. We systematically continued the process until all possible combinations were listed.

Evaluate the Results

It would be possible to eat twenty-four days in a row at Hamburger Heaven and never eat the same meal twice—UGH! This type of combination problem applies to many of our everyday activities. When we get dressed in the morning, we choose from a limited number of items, yet even a modest wardrobe offers a huge number of possible combinations.

The final question in the problem leads to a more important discovery. If we added one more burger, how many additional meals could we construct? Observing our list above, notice that each burger is included in eight meals. One more burger should add a similar number. Looking a bit further, if we include an additional fry (extra greasy) we add twelve meals. One extra drink increases the number of meals by only six.

One final observation is perhaps the most surprising. Notice that the total number of combinations is equal to the product of the number of items in each column. In this case:

Original menu—$3 \times 2 \times 4 = 24$

This explains how the number of meals grows.

Add one burger—$4 \times 2 \times 4 = 32$ (adds 8 meals)
Add one fry—$3 \times 3 \times 4 = 36$ (adds 12 meals)
Add one drink—$3 \times 2 \times 5 = 30$ (adds 6 meals)

Does this pattern always work? What happens when a fourth column (dessert) is included? Set your class to work on extending their understanding of combinations. They will eat it up! (See "Ice-Cream Expert," page 65.)

LIST OF MEALS

Meal	Hamburger	Fry	Drink
1	BB (Boring Burger)	FF (French Fries)	OG (Orange)
2	BB	FF	CK (Cola)
3	BB	FF	RB (Root Beer)
4	BB	FF	ML (Milk)
5	BB	OR (Onion Rings)	OG
6	BB	OR	CK
7	BB	OR	RB
8	BB	OR	ML
9	KB (Kiloburger)	FF	OG
10	KB	FF	CK
11	KB	FF	RB
12	KB	FF	ML
13	KB	OR	OG
14	KB	OR	CK
15	KB	OR	RB
16	KB	OR	ML
17	FM (Fat Burger)	FF	OG
18	FM	FF	CK
19	FM	FF	RB
20	FM	FF	ML
21	FM	OR	OG
22	FM	OR	CK
23	FM	OR	RB
24	FM	OR	ML

Problem and Solution 30

POPCORN TRUTH

(Problem Starter Sheet 30, page 126)

Companies are always advertising that their product is better than the rest. "Our toothpaste makes your teeth whiter"; "Kids eat more Corn Puffies than any other cereal." Ever wonder if the commercials are true? Here is an ad for you to test out for yourself: "You pay a little more, but our popcorn leaves fewer unpopped kernels, so it's a better buy."

Go to the store and buy the same-sized bag of the *most* expensive and *least* expensive popcorn. Do an experiment to find out if the expensive popcorn is actually a better buy.

Solution: Popcorn Truth

Understand the Problem

   Facts

   • We have two brands of popcorn.

   Conditions

   • Brand X costs more than Brand Y.

   • Brand X is supposed to pop more completely than Brand Y.

   Goal

   • Find if Brand X is a better buy than Brand Y.

Select a Strategy

Students can count out 250 kernels of Brand X and Y in separate paper bags and then pop each brand in a microwave for the same amount of time. They can count the number of unpopped kernels and record in a table. Last, they can compare the difference in popping efficiency to the initial cost.

Carry Out the Strategy

This experiment could be carried out in school or at home. Provide a sufficient supply of Brand X and Y popcorn so students can work in pairs or in small groups. The activity works best in a classroom when set up as a learning center and made available throughout the day.

Because each region of the country will have different brands of popcorn to investigate, the following is offered as an example only. Suppose we bought two bags of popcorn:

Popcorn	Cost
Brand X—250 grams	$1.40
Band T—250 grams	$1.00

Popping 250 kernels of each brand for four minutes gave the following results.

POPPING RESULTS

	Number of Kernels	Number of Remaining Kernels	Failure Rate
Brand X	250	8	3.2%
Brand Y	250	37	14.8%

Out of 250 kernels, Brand X had 8 remaining and Brand Y had 37 remaining. The percent failure is the number remaining divided by the total number of kernels. For example, if 1 out of 100 kernels didn't pop, the failure rate would be:

$$1 \div 100 = .01 \text{ or } 1\%$$

Encourage students to use a calculator to carry out these computations.

Evaluate the Results

Certainly the expensive Brand X has a lower failure rate (3.2%) as compared to Brand Y (14.8%). But are the rates different enough to compensate for the higher initial price?

First let's determine how much "poppable" corn we actually purchased. Out of 250 grams, if we assume the failure rates above are reasonably accurate, only part of the corn we bought is eatable.

Original Amount	Failure Rate	Unpoppable Corn	Eatable Corn
Brand X 250 grams	3.2%	8 grams	242 grams
Brand Y 250 grams	14.8%	37 grams	213 grams

So of the amount purchased, only 242 grams of Brand X and 213 grams of Brand Y are eatable. To determine the actual cost per gram of eatable corn, we divide the total price by the number of grams. For example, if 10 cents buys 5 grams, each gram costs 2 cents (10 ÷ 5 = 2). Therefore,

	Total Cost	Eatable Amount	Price/ Gram
Brand X	$1.40	242 grams	$.0057
Brand Y	$1.00	213 grams	$.0046

Even with a lower failure rate, Brand X costs about a tenth of a cent more per gram than Brand Y. (Note that $.0057 is a bit more than ½ cent, .0046 is a bit less than ½ cent.) In fact, even if Brand X had a zero failure rate (all the kernels popped) the failure rate for Brand Y would have to double (28%) before it would become more "expensive."

Other consumer-oriented experiments can be designed to test claims about paper towels, liquid detergent, and hand soaps. Problem solving in the marketplace is a valuable skill.

Problem and Solution 31

COW THOUGHTS

(Problem Starter Sheet 31, page 127)
Pico Steerman, a well-known rancher, invented a new style of corral for his cattle. By driving a herd of steers through gate A, the cow-doctor could check them one at a time for disease at Exit B.

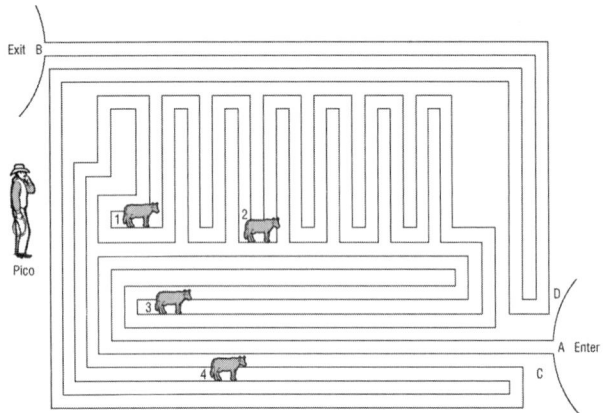

Sometimes a stray cow wanders into the maze through the openings at C or D, and though it appears to be trapped in the coral, it is actually free. Help Pico, who is standing outside the corral, figure out a way to quickly determine which steers are inside the corral and which are free to roam the range. Can you figure out a method that will always work, regardless of the position of the cow or how complex the maze? Remember, Pico can't look down on the corral, as shown in the picture above.

Solution: Cow Thoughts
Understand the Problem
Facts
- Cows are either inside or outside the corral.

Conditions
- The corral must be one region (i.e., one corral), or cows couldn't go completely through to exit.
- An observer on the outside must be able to determine whether a cow is *inside* or *free* without being able to view possible paths to freedom (you would need a helicopter so you could look down from above).

Goal
- Find a quick method to determine if a cow is safely inside the corral or is free.

Select a Strategy
Have students simplify the problem situation by starting with a very simple corral. If they imagine themselves standing outside looking at a cow inside, how many fences are between them and the cow? They can try the same procedure with the cow outside. They can continue this process with more and more complicated corrals, organize the results in a table, and look for a pattern.

Carry Out the Strategy
Have students start with a simple corral.

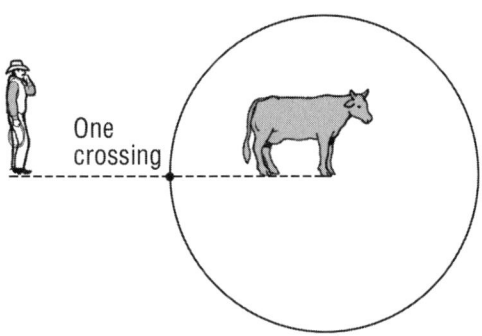

If the cow is inside, there is always exactly one fence between you and the cow.

If the cow is outside, there can be either zero or two fences between you and the cow.

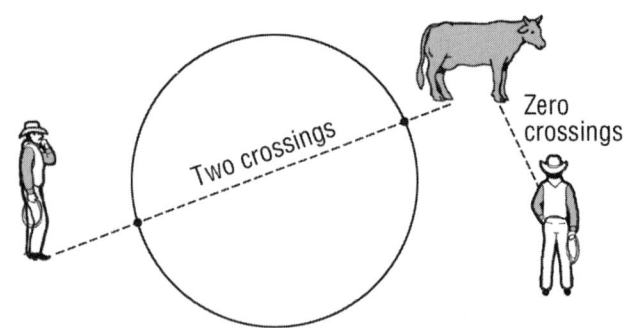

Note: If the line of sight falls along the edge of the fence and students don't know whether to count it as zero, one, or two crossings, they can move a bit to one side until the situation becomes clear.

A slightly more complicated corral adds more information to the situation.

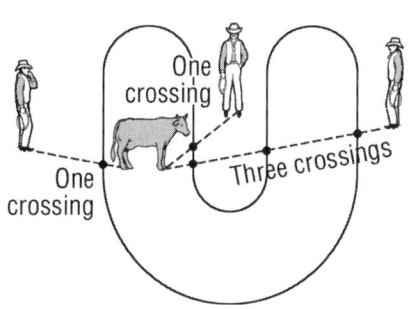

If the cow is inside, there are one or three fence crossings. If the cow is outside, there are zero, two, or four crossings.

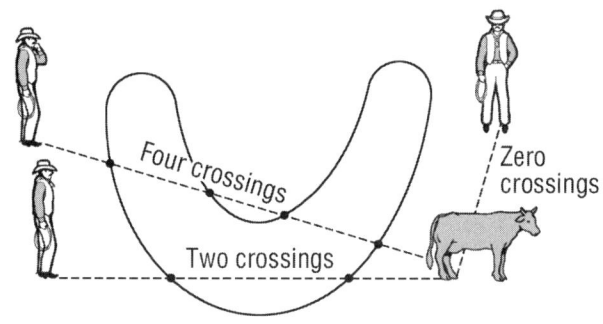

These and the results of several other experiments are organized in the table below. Search for patterns.

NUMBER OF FENCE CROSSINGS

Corral	Cow Inside	Cow Outside
1	1	0 or 2
2	1 or 3	0 or 2 or 4
3	1, 3, or 5	0 or 2 or 4 or 6
4	1 or 3 or 5 or 7	0 or 2 or 4 or 6 or 8

Evaluate the Results

A clear pattern emerges in the table above. If the cow is inside, there seems to be an odd number of fences between the observer and the cow. If outside, an even number of fence crossings will be noted.

We can help Pico solve his problem by suggesting that he simply count the number of fences between himself and any cow of interest. If there are an odd number of crossings, he has nothing to worry about. However, if the number turns up even, Pico has a

loose cow on his hands. Therefore, in Pico's corral, cows 1 and 3 are outside, 2 and 4 inside.

An interesting magic trick can be performed based on this same principle. You need a piece of string approximately 2 meters long. Tie the ends of the string together to form a long loop. On a smooth table, place your finger inside the loop and pull it into a complicated, snake-like pattern. Make sure the string doesn't cross over itself anywhere. Remember the spot where your finger was when you constructed the string maze. Now have an observer place a finger anywhere inside the pattern. You instantly report whether the finger is inside our outside the loop. When pulled, his finger will either be caught or the loop will neatly slip away.

The trick is to quickly count the number of string crossings between the observer's finger and the spot where your finger was when you completed the loop pattern. If the number is even, the observer's finger will be caught; if odd, it will be outside the loop. An even more dramatic exercise involves your carefully placing all five fingers of the observer's hand in such a way that there are exactly two strings between each finger. When the loop is pulled, all five fingers will either be caught or the loop will pull cleanly away. Such magic!

Problem and Solution 32

CLASSROOM MANEUVERS

(Problem Starter Sheet 32, page 128)
Mr. Nitpicker's classroom is organized in five neat rows with five desks in each row. The desks are separated so you can walk in front and behind, as well as between them.

Arthur and the teacher are standing as in the picture. What is the shortest route for Arthur to walk in order to ask Mr. Nitpicker for the hall pass?

Here are two possible routes:

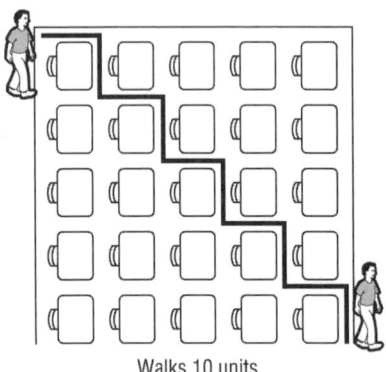

Walks 10 units

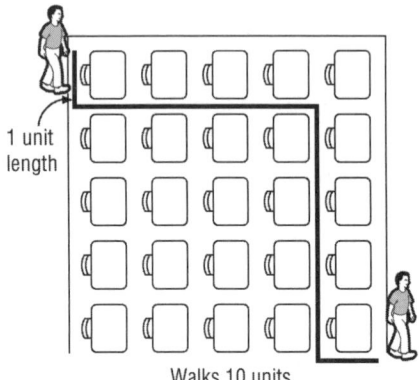

1 unit length

Walks 10 units

Solution: Classroom Maneuvers

Understand the Problem

Facts

- There are five rows of desks with five in each row.
- The desks are evenly spaced so you can walk in front, behind, and between them.
- Arthur and the teacher are on opposite corners of the classroom.

Conditions

- Arthur must walk between desks (no jumping over).
- The desks must be close enough together so that you must make sharp turns.

Goal

- Find the shortest route from Arthur to Mr. Nitpicker.

Select a Strategy

Using centimeter-squared paper, students can make several five-unit squares. Using these simplified model sketches, they can conduct several experiments and record the route lengths and then look for a pattern.

Carry Out the Strategy

Here are several different routes:

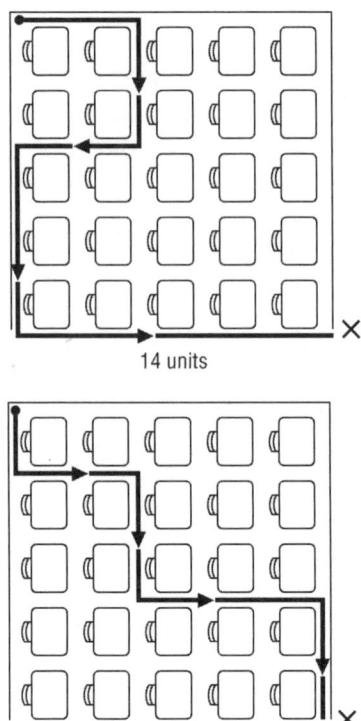

14 units

10 units

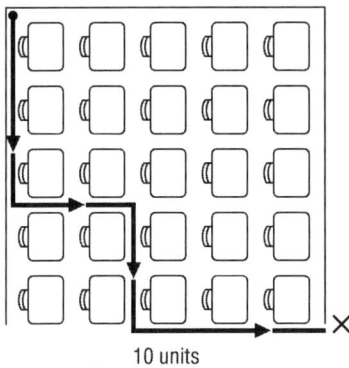

10 units

Evaluate the Results

Careful observation of these sketches should show that as long as Arthur moves to the right and toward the front, he will always walk exactly ten units. Only when he doubles back (as in the first example) will the route require extra steps.

As an extension to this problem, it might be interesting to figure out the total number of different ten-unit routes. Start with a square with one unit on a side:

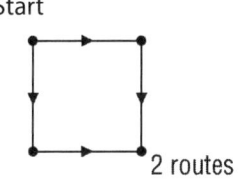

Then look at a 2×2 square (numbers indicate the number of routes to any point). If there is one way to get to point a and two to b, then there must be three ways to c. Therefore, there are six routes to point d.

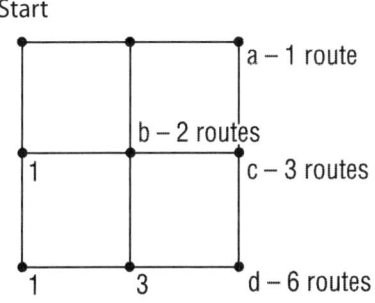

Similarly, for a 3×3 square:

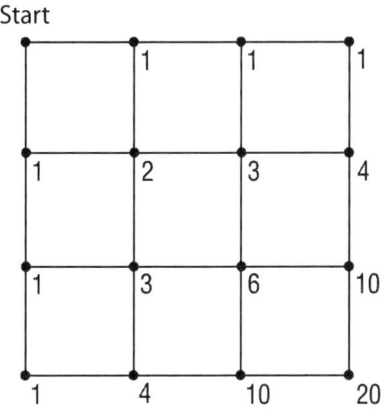

Continuing the process gives us:

Length of Edge	Number of Minimum Routes
1	2
2	6
3	20
4	70
5	252

Arthur could take a new route each day and still have plenty left over by the end of the school year!

Problem and Solution 33

THE PURLOINED SAPPHIRE

(Problem Starter Sheet 33, page 129)

Inspector Chang was called in to investigate the case of the missing sapphire. The gem was the centerpiece of a beautiful fountain in the middle of a courtyard. There were four rooms opening onto the courtyard, so one of four people staying in these rooms must have been responsible. But which one?

The only clue was the track of footprints left by the thief when he got his or her feet wet removing the sapphire. The thief left the path below, hoping to confuse the investigation. Chang took one look at the trail and immediately pointed at the person in room C as the culprit. How did she know for sure?

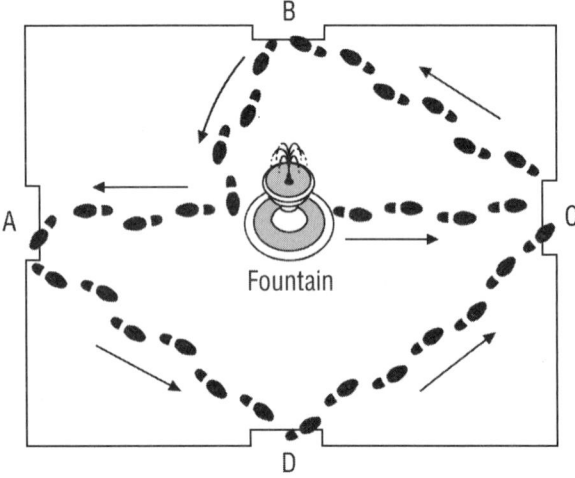

Solution: The Purloined Sapphire

Understand the Problem

Facts

- The gem was taken from the fountain.
- The thief got wet stealing the gem so the footprints start at the fountain.
- The thief left a complicated trail of wet footprints from door to door, hoping to confuse the investigation.

Conditions

- The thief was in a hurry so he or she couldn't retrace his steps. (He or she could walk backward, however.)
- The thief had to end up in his or her own room.

- The footprints were discovered before they dried up.

Goal

- By observing only the path of the crime, determine which room (A, B, C, or D) contained the culprit.

Select a Strategy

Students can make a simple sketch of the courtyard arrangement and the footprint path. They can try starting at the fountain and follow the path to see where it ends. It might be useful to design several networks, organize the results in a table, and look for a pattern.

Carry Out the Strategy

Using a simple diagram of the courtyard, have students trace several different paths.

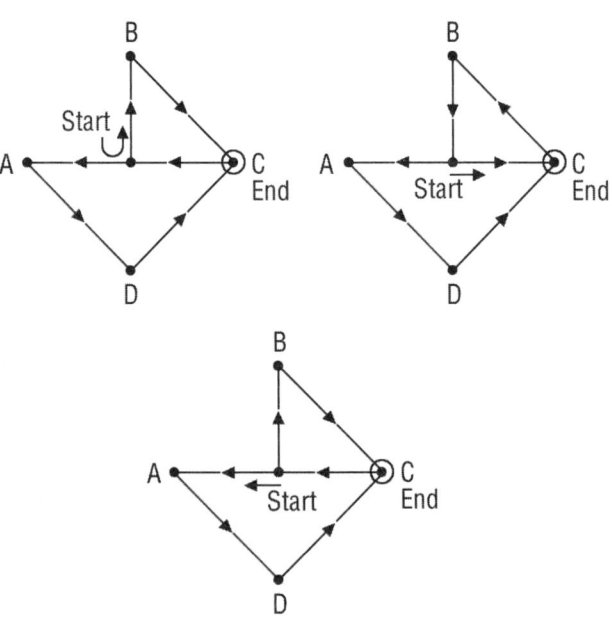

Evaluate the Results

A clear pattern should be apparent. If you start at the fountain (center dot) and you always end up at C! Also observe that only room C and the fountain are points where three paths come together. All other points connect only two paths. Chang learned about network problems in a topology course she had taken in college, so she knew that if you start at a point where an odd number of paths come together, you cannot end there.

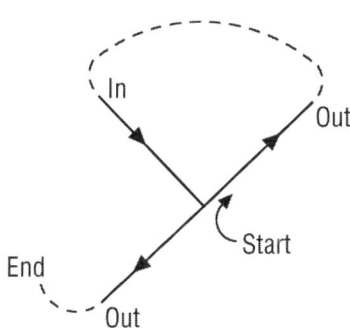

However, if you don't start at an odd vertex, you must end there.

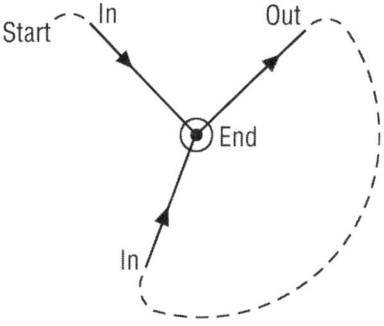

The opposite is true for even vertices. If you start at an even vertex, you must end there.

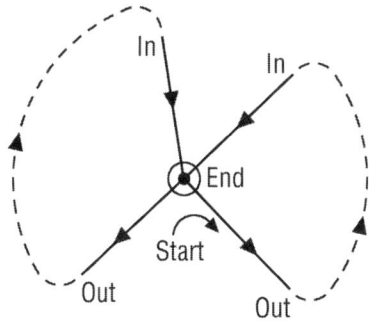

If you do not start at an even vertex, you cannot end there.

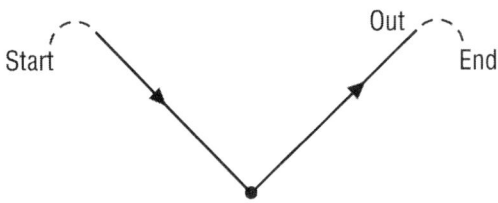

As a follow-up activity, prepare several networks and have your class determine which can be traversed without retracing any paths. See if they can discover the rule that predicts whether a figure is "traceable" without repeating a path. Suggest that each student sketch a figure and exchange with a friend to see if it is traceable. The results make excellent bulletin boards. (See Problem 34, "Line'ardo DaVinci," on page 78.)

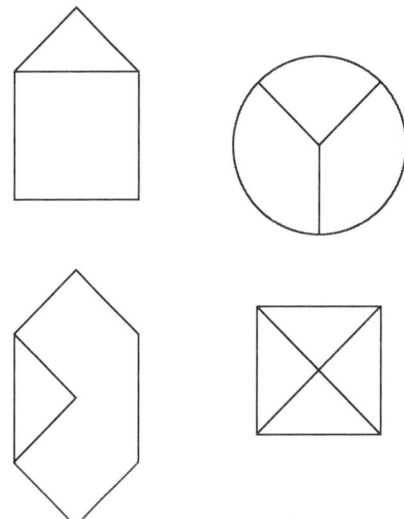

A network is traceable if it contains exactly zero or two odd vertices. If a figure has two odd vertices, start at one and finish at the other. If it has no odd vertices, start anywhere and end at the same point.

It is also fun to investigate three-dimensional figures where edges become the paths and corners the vertices. Do the same rules apply?

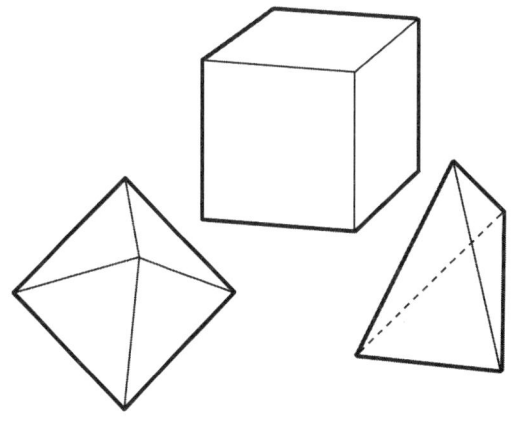

Problem and Solution 34

LINE'ARDO DAVINCI

(Problem Starter Sheet 34, page 130)

Line'ardo paints the white line down the middle of the road in his county. He is trying to conserve fuel, so he checks out his map each morning to plan his shortest route. Can Line'ardo "line" all the roads connecting the four cities below without retracing any routes? If so, where should he start?

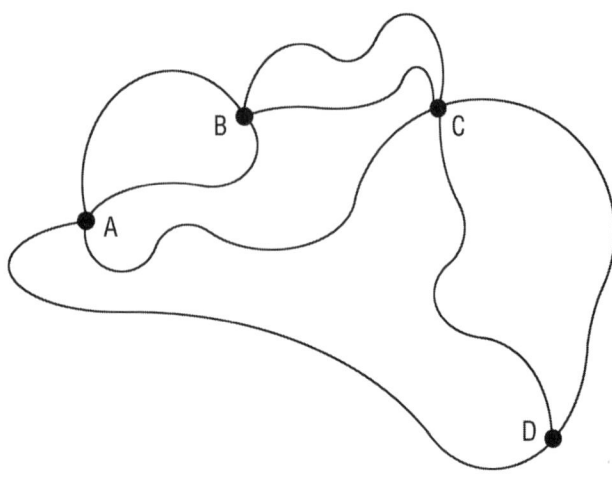

Solution: Line'Ardo DaVinci

Understand the Problem

Facts
- Four cities (A, B, C, and D) are connected by roads.
- Line'ardo must pass over every road.

Conditions
- He cannot retrace his route.
- He cannot travel from one city to another without going along a road.

Goal
- Traverse all the routes connecting the four cities without retracing any roads.

Select a Strategy

Students can construct a simplified drawing of the map. They can then experiment with various routes by tracing the simplified figure with a pencil. Have them arrange the results in a table.

Carry Out the Strategy

The figure below is an identical, though simpler, arrangement of the cities and connecting roads.

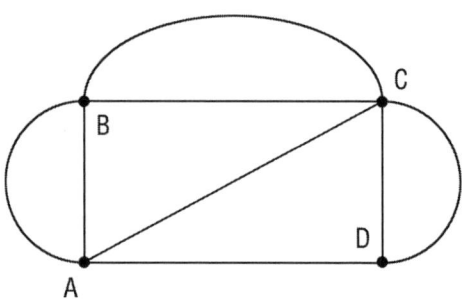

Have students try to trace the figure beginning at A.

Not Traceable

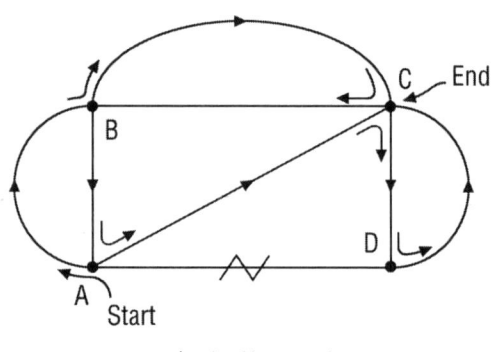

$\bigwedge$ = Untraced

Not Traceable

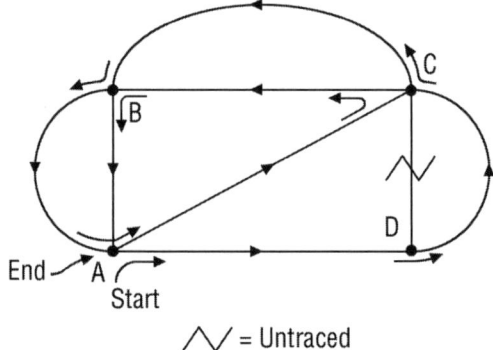

$\bigwedge$ = Untraced

Conduct several experiments beginning at each city. Organize the results in a table.

Start	Traceable	End
A	No	C
A	No	A
A	No	D
B	No	A
B	No	C
C	Yes	D
C	Yes	D
D	Yes	C
D	Yes	C
D	Yes	C

A network is traceable if it contains exactly zero or two odd vertices. If a figure has two odd vertices, start at one and end at the other. If it has no odd vertices, start anywhere and end at the same point.

Evaluate the Results

Notice that complete routes are not possible when starting at A or B. Almost any route starting at C or D is traceable. If Line'ardo starts at C, he will have dinner at D and vice versa. Try other networks of routes connecting 3, 4, 5, or more cities. Keep track of the even and odd vertices (number of routes coming together at a point). Can your students discover the rule for traceability? (See "The Purloined Sapphire," Starter Sheet 33.)

Problem and Solution 35

JAILHOUSE BLUES

(Problem Starter Sheet 35, page 131)

John Turnkey, the prison warden, decided to free his prisoners for good behavior. The cells were numbered from 1 to 25. Each had a lock that opened when you turned it once and locked when it was turned again, and so on.

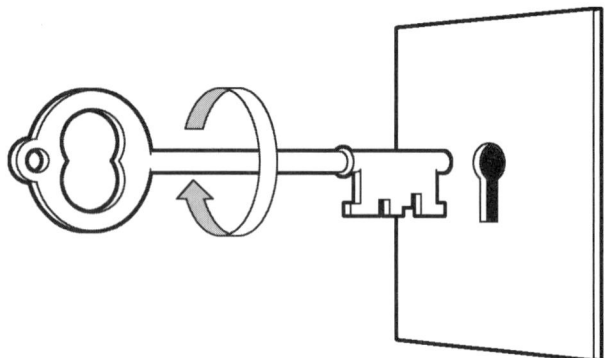

One night when the prisoners were sleeping, he quietly turned all the locks once, opening all the cells. He began to worry that he may have freed too many prisoners, so he went back and turned every second lock (2, 4, 6, 8, . . . 24), which locked half the cells. Thinking that there still might be too many prisoners freed, he gave every third lock a turn (3, 6, 9, 12, . . . 24), then every fourth lock (4, 8, 12, . . . 24), fifth (5, 10, 15, 20, 25), sixth (6, 12, 18, 24), seventh, eight, ninth, tenth, eleventh, and so on all the way to every twenty-fifth (of course, he only turned one lock for every thirteenth cell and above).

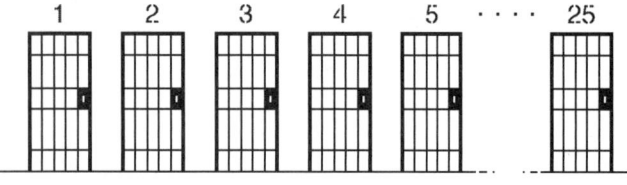

Who got out of jail in the morning?

Solution: Jailhouse Blues

Understand the Problem

Facts

- There are twenty-five jail cells.
- The locks open with first turn, close on the next turn, and so on.

Conditions

- The warden first opens all locks, then turns even-numbered locks (multiples of 2), then every third lock, then multiples of 4, 5, 6, 7, 8, 9, 10, 11, all the way up to multiples of 25.
- Only one lock is turned for multiples of 13, 14, 15, …25.
- Each pass through the prison may open some cells and lock others.

Goal

- Find which cells will be open after the above process is completed.

Select a Strategy

Students can construct a list of cell numbers and keep track of each turn with a check mark below the appropriate cell numbers. After completing the twenty-five passes through the cells, they can determine the total number of turns for each cell and then look for a pattern to determine who is free.

Carry Out the Strategy

The table on the next page gives a summary of twenty-five passes through the jail turning the locks as described above.

Evaluate the Results

First, let's observe the relationship between the number of turns and whether a lock is open or closed.

> 1 turn—open
> 2 turns—closed
> 3 turns—open
> 4 turns—closed
> 5 turns—open
> 6 turns—closed
> and so on….

Notice that an odd number of times opens the lock; an even number closes it. Therefore the results listed in the table show that prisoners in cells 1, 4, 9, 16, and 25 will be freed.

Cell numbers

Multiple of	1	2	3	4	5	6	7	8	9	10	11	12	13	14	15	16	17	18	19	20	21	22	23	24	25
1	✓	✓	✓	✓	✓	✓	✓	✓	✓	✓	✓	✓	✓	✓	✓	✓	✓	✓	✓	✓	✓	✓	✓	✓	✓
2		✓		✓		✓		✓		✓		✓		✓		✓		✓		✓		✓		✓	
3			✓			✓			✓			✓			✓			✓			✓			✓	
4				✓				✓				✓				✓				✓				✓	
5					✓					✓					✓					✓					✓
6						✓						✓						✓						✓	
7							✓							✓							✓				
8								✓								✓								✓	
9									✓									✓							
10										✓										✓					
11											✓											✓			
12												✓												✓	
13													✓												
14														✓											
15															✓										
16																✓									
17																	✓								
18																		✓							
19																			✓						
20																				✓					
21																					✓				
22																						✓			
23																							✓		
24																								✓	
25																									✓
Total turns	1 Open	2	2	3 Open	2	4	2	4	3 Open	4	2	6	2	4	4	5 Open	2	6	2	6	4	4	2	8	3 Open

It is interesting to note that the data collected for our jailhouse problem are identical to counting the factors for a given number. For example, 12 has six factors: 1, 2, 3, 4, 6, 12. Six is also the number of lock turns for cell 12. To find out who is freed, we simply look for numbers with an odd number of factors—the square numbers. For example, 16 has five factors: 1, 2, 4, 8, 16. Notice that only square numbers (1, 4, 9, 16, 25 . . .) have an odd number of fractions. Why? Developing a general rule that solves this problem demonstrates the power of mathematics to extend solutions to more general cases. Have your class use this general rule to find out who would get out of jail if there were 100 cells; 1,000 cells.

Problem and Solution 36

BILL YUD POOL

(Problem Starter Sheet 36, page 132)

Bill Yud was an avid pool player. He enjoyed impressing his friends with his feats of skill. He invented a new pool table that could be adjusted to almost any size and had pockets in only three of the four corners. Someone could call out any size table and old Bill would think for a minute and then point to one of the pockets. Next he would place the ball in the lower-left corner and shoot out at a 45° angle. That ball would scoot all over the table and sure enough would fall into the chosen pocket. He never missed! Can you figure out what Bill was up to? Here are a few examples.

Table – 3 x 5

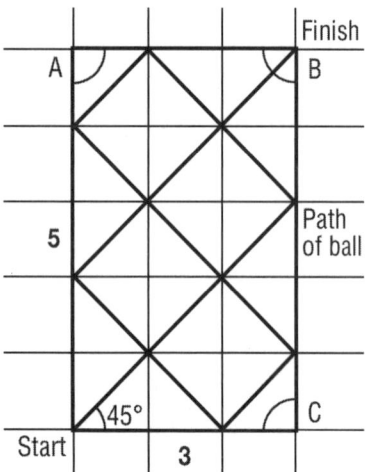

Table – 4 x 7

Solution: Bill Yud Pool
Understand the Problem
   Facts
   - The table has three pockets; length and width of table varies.
   - The ball bounces off an edge at the same angle it strikes.

Conditions
   - Shoot out from the lower left-hand corner (no pocket) at 45°.
   - You must hit the ball hard enough so it continues to roll until it reaches a pocket.

Goal
   - Predict which pocket (A, B, or C) the ball will end in.

Select a Strategy
Using graph paper, students can play several "Bill Yud" games and organize the results in a table.

From *Solving Math Problems Kids Care About*. Copyright © 2006 Good Year Books.

Carry Out the Strategy

Here is the record of twelve experiments.

Ball Ends in Pocket	A	B	C
Table (length, height)	(5, 6)	(3, 5)	(4, 7)
	(3, 4)	(5, 7)	(4, 6)
	(3, 6)	(4, 4)	(2, 3)
	(1, 2)	(2, 14)	(4, 5)

Initially no clear patterns become apparent. However, with a bit more experimenting we see that some games leave the same shape "track." For example, (4, 6) and (2,3) are identical games but are different size scales.

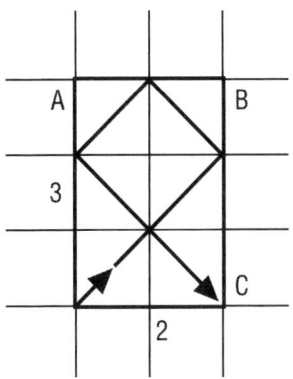

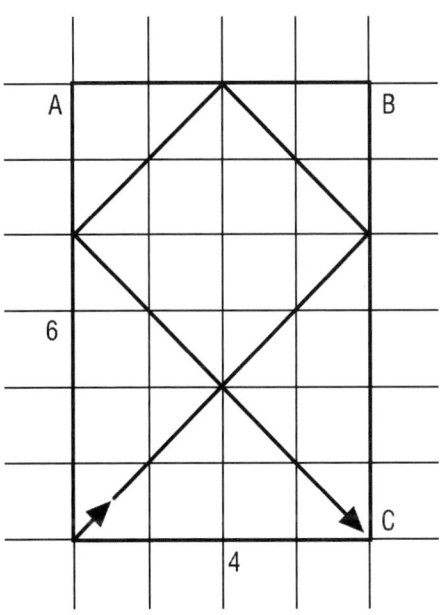

Therefore, if (2,3) ends at C, then (4, 6) must end at C as well. And what about (6, 9), (8, 12), and (10, 15)? Because this whole "family" of games ends at C, it is only necessary to include the simplest (2,3) in the table. Similarly, this is true for (1, 2) and (3, 6) in column A and (1, 7) and (2, 14) in column B.

Ball Ends in Pocket	A	B	C
Simplest Table	(5, 6)	(3, 5)	(4, 7)
(length, height)	(3, 4)	(5, 7)	(2, 3)
	(1, 2)	(1, 1)	(2, 3)
	(1, 2)	(1, 7)	(4, 5)

Evaluate the Results

A clear pattern now emerges. Every "table" in column A has an odd length and even height. The opposite is true for C. Tables in column B have an odd length and width.

Test this pattern to see if it always works. Many times the rule will hold only for selected cases and will require modification after additional experimentation. In this case, the pattern holds for all "simple" tables (i.e., dimensions are relatively prime). Other tables must have their dimensions reduced (rescaled) before the prediction works consistently.

Additional problems of interest include:

1. Which games have a track that crosses every square?
2. Can you predict how many times the ball touches the edge of the table? (Count the starting and ending points.)
3. What happens when you use triangular or circular tables?

Problem and Solution 37

FARMING A FIELD

(Problem Starter Sheet 37, page 133)

A farmer needs to know how much area his fields cover so he can buy the correct amount of seed and fertilizer. Aggie McDonald's farm has trees planted in a regular square pattern. Aggie's grandfather planted the trees years ago to help him compute the area of various-shaped fields for planting.

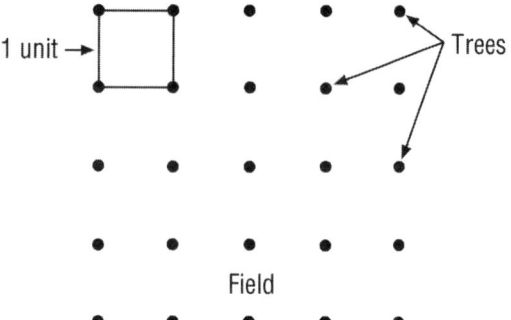

Aggie liked to plant interesting shaped fields of corn, beans, and squash. (Rectangular fields can be a bit boring to plow.) Can you use the tree pattern to help Aggie figure out the areas of these fields in unit squares? (A "unit" is the area of the small squares formed by the tree pattern.)

1.
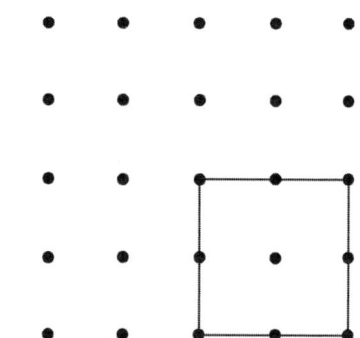

2.

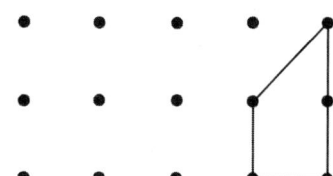

3.
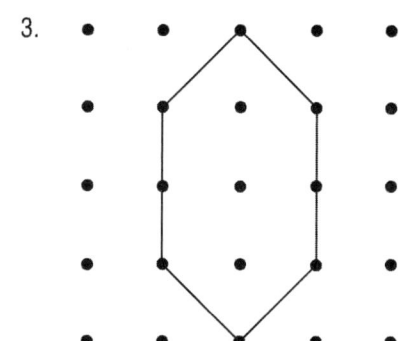

4.
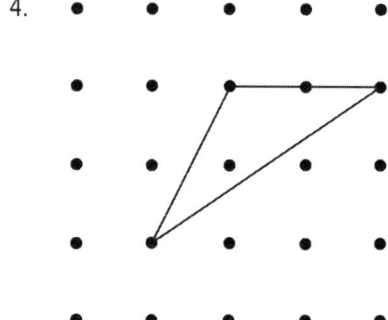

Try some other shapes. Can you find the area of any field? (Make sure the corners lie on a tree; only straight edges, please.)

Solution: Farming a Field

Understand the Problem

Facts

- The trees form a pattern of equal squares on the field.
- A unit square is a square formed by four adjacent trees.

Conditions

- The corners of figures must lie on a tree.
- The sides of fields must be straight lines.

Goal

- Find areas of various fields in unit squares.

Select a Strategy

Students can use a geoboard or dot paper as a model for the farm. Then they can break the problem into smaller parts or add something to the problem situation to ease solution.

Carry Out the Strategy

Have students construct the first shape on the geoboard or graph paper.

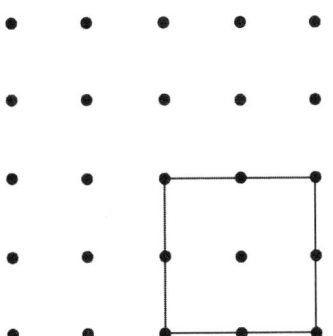

By breaking up the problem into smaller parts, the solution is easy to calculate (1 + 1 + 1 + 1 = 4 unit squares).

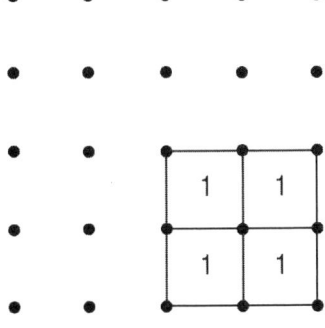

By adding a few lines to the second problem, the solution is fairly transparent.

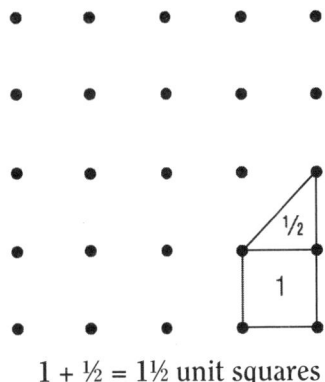

1 + ½ = 1½ unit squares

Similarly,

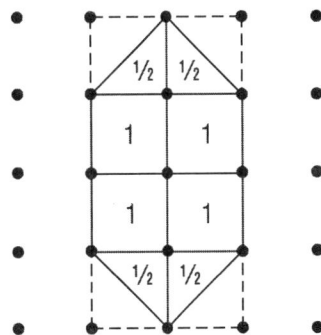

1 + 1 + 1 + 1 + ½ + ½ + ½ + ½ = 6 unit squares

The last example cannot be easily broken into parts. Instead we fit a rectangle around the outside and see what we must "tear" off to arrive at the original figure.

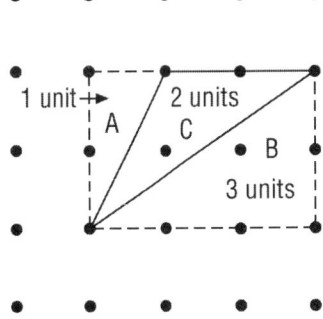

C = 6 − 1 − 3 = 2 unit squares

The whole rectangle has an area of six units. Triangle A is one half of 2 units (1 unit). Triangle B is one-half of the whole rectangle (3 units). So the original triangle C = 6 − 1 − 3 = 2 unit squares.

Problem 5 is by far the most interesting (and most time-consuming) of this set. Its solution requires gathering lots of experimental data. Tables are extremely useful in organizing the data and searching for patterns. The two key variables are:

1. The number of trees (nails) on the edge of figure (E).
2. The number of trees (nails) completely inside the field (I).

Note: Identifyling variables may require considerable experimentation.

The following table shows the result of your experimentation.

INSIDE NAILS (I)

(Area in unit squares)

Edge Nails (E)	0	1	2	3	4	5
3	½	1½	2½	3½	4½	5½
4	1	2	3	4	?	?
5	1½	2½	3½	4½	?	?
6	2	3	4	5	?	?
7	2½	?	?	?	?	?
8	?	?	?	?	?	?

Evaluate the Results

The table can be extended based on the discovered patterns and each new item tested for accuracy. Some students may even describe rules that describe these patterns. For example:

1. As you put one more nail inside (I), the area gets one unit bigger.
2. As you add one nail to the edge (E) without changing the number inside, the area gets bigger by ½ unit.

The mathematical function that summarizes the entire relationship is:

$$\tfrac{1}{2} E + I - 1 = Area$$

Check to see if this formula always works. For example, with 6 nails on the edge and 2 inside, we have:

$$(\tfrac{1}{2} \times 6 + 2) - 1 = (3 + 2) - 1$$
$$= 5 - 1 = 4 \text{ unit squares.}$$

Once the general rule is thoroughly understood, previous techniques of breaking up or adding to the problem situation are unnecessary. Additional problems of interest might include finding areas of fields on a triangular geoboard.

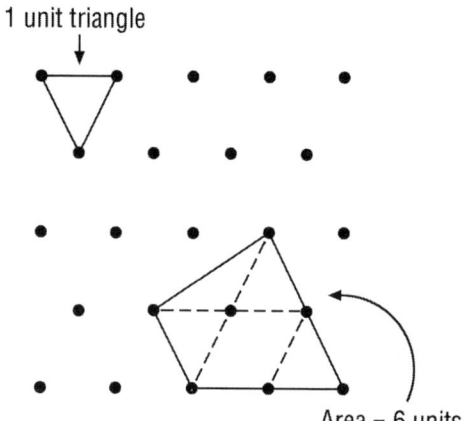

1 unit triangle

Area = 6 units

Problem and Solution 38

CLYDE THE CLASS CLOWN

(Problem Starter Sheet 38, page 134)

One day Clyde got caught putting a toad in Mrs. Purdy's purse. For days he didn't get called on to take the lunch count to the office. He spent the whole weekend trying to figure out a solution for his problem. Early Monday morning he asked Mrs. Purdy if she would pick the class messenger in the following way:

After attendance, everyone sits in a circle with the teacher in the center. Each counts off one at a time (1, 2, 3, 4, ...). Once everyone has a number, the teacher begins sending children to their seats by skipping number 1, sending number 2, skipping number 3, sending number 4, and so on until she goes around the circle completely. She doesn't stop, however, and continues skipping every other student until only one is left. This lucky person gets to take the lunch count to the office. If there are ten students in the class, number 5 will be chosen.

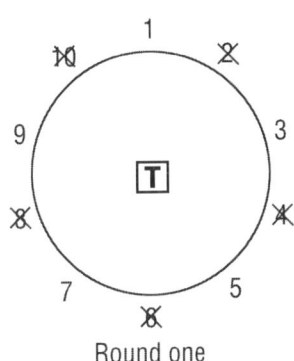

Round one

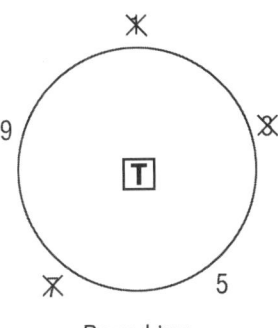

Round two

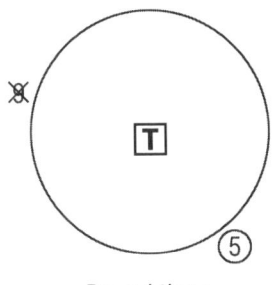

Round three

Where should Clyde sit if there are eleven students? Twelve students? Fifteen students? Twenty students? Thirty students? Can you find a rule that works for any size class?

Solution: Clyde the Class Clown

Understand the Problem

Facts

- Students count off clockwise (1, 2, 3, ...). Students are eliminated by skipping every other one and continuing around the circle until only one is left.
- Don't skip the number 1 position on each subsequent round unless the last person was eliminated.

Condition

- The total number of students is known before anyone sits down.

Goal

- Find where Clyde should sit if he doesn't want to be eliminated.

Select a Strategy

Students can simplify the problem by sketching circles for all the class sizes from one to twenty. They can conduct experiments, organize the results in a table, and look for a pattern.

Carry Out the Strategy

The sketches on the next page show class sizes from one to eight. The Xs show the students sent to their seats. The circled position number is the one remaining.

Class Size	"Lucky Pattern"
1	1
2	1
3	3
4	1
5	3
6	5
7	7
8	1
9	3
10	5
11	7
12	9
13	11
14	13
15	15
16	1
17	3
18	5

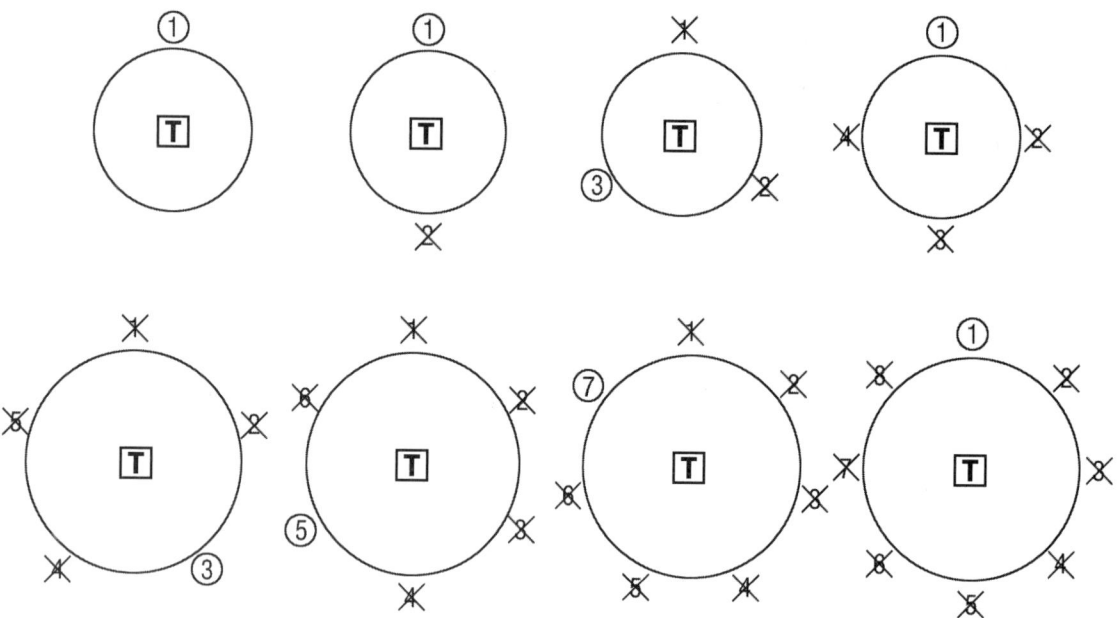

Evaluate the Results

The lucky position is always an odd number. Looking at the table, notice that if the class size is one, two, four, eight, or sixteen students, the lucky position is number 1. For each class size between these key numbers, the lucky position can be found by counting off using odd numbers. For example, if there are twenty-four students, the largest key number is 16. For each number (16 through 24), count off odd numbers until you reach 24: 1 (16), 3 (17), 5 (18), 7 (19), 9 (20), 11 (21), 13 (22), 15 (23), 17 (24). For twenty-four students the lucky position is number 17.

If your class is bigger than thirty-one students (and whose isn't these days?), you will find the next key number is 32 (lucky position number 1). Notice that the key numbers seem to grow by a doubling process.

This sequence is also known as the "powers of two": 2^0, 2^1, 2^2, 2^3, 2^4, $2^{5,}$ . . . What is the next key number after 32? (See "Stack the Deck," page 57, for a similar problem.)

Problem and Solution 39

THE BICYCLE DILEMMA

(Problem Starter Sheet, page 135)
Cary rode her bicycle to the pet store after school every day to help clean the bird cages. There was only one bike rack near the store and Cary noticed it was full about half the time. She tried to convince the shop owner to put in one more rack so she wouldn't have to worry about losing her bike while she was working.

With one bike rack Cary can lock up her bike four out of eight times she works. On the average, how many out of every eight working days would she find a parking space if a second rack were installed?

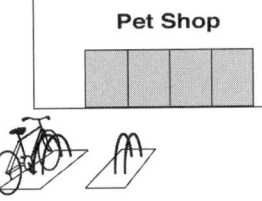

Pet Shop

Solution: The Bicycle Dilemma

Understand the Problem

Fact
• One bike rack is being used half the time.

Condition
• Assume there are enough bicycles so that the rack is filled half the time.

Goal
• Determine how many days out of eight that a rack will be free if a second rack is installed.

Select a Strategy

This problem is equivalent to flipping one or two coins. When flipping a coin, heads and tails each appear about half the time. When flipping two coins, each still has a fifty-fifty chance of coming up heads or tails. Mathematicians say the coin problem "models" the bike rack problem.

In this case, heads might represent a full rack and tails an empty rack.

Students can conduct an experiment by flipping one coin 100 times and record the number of heads and tails in a table. Then have them do the same with two coins, keeping track of heads and tails of both coins.

Carry Out the Strategy

The following table shows a record of 100 flips of a single coin:

One-coin Experiment

Heads	Tails
~~1111~~	~~1111~~
~~1111~~	~~1111~~
~~1111~~	~~1111~~
~~1111~~	~~1111~~
~~1111~~	~~1111~~
~~1111~~	~~1111~~
~~1111~~	~~1111~~
~~1111~~	~~1111~~
~~1111~~	~~1111~~
1111	~~1111~~ 1
49	**51**

For two coins there are three possible outcomes:

Two-Coin Experiment

Both Heads	Both Tails	Heads & Tails
~~1111~~ ~~1111~~	~~1111~~ ~~1111~~	~~1111~~ ~~1111~~
~~1111~~ ~~1111~~	~~1111~~ ~~1111~~	~~1111~~ ~~1111~~
~~1111~~ 1	~~1111~~	~~1111~~ ~~1111~~
		~~1111~~ ~~1111~~
		~~1111~~ 1111
26	**25**	**49**

Evaluate the Results

Notice that the results in the first experiment confirm our expectations that we should get heads about half the time. This result is equivalent to one bike rack being full half the time.

The results using two coins are more interesting. If tails represents a vacant bike rack, both columns two and three above will offer Cary an empty bike rack. Only the "both heads" column leaves no space available to lock her bike. Out of 100 flips of two coins, 74 coins (about three-fourths) provide at least one tail (open bike rack). On the average, then, Cary should find an open rack approximately three-fourths of the time, or six out of eight days.

Without doing an experiment of this type, it is easy to assume that because there are enough bicycles around to keep all the bike racks full about half the time, the chances of finding a free rack should remain the same—about one-half, or 50 percent. The two-coin experiment exposes this false assumption.

Your students might be interested in investigating the situation with three, four, or five available bike racks. Just use 3, 4, or 5 coins and start flipping. A word of caution: This problem quickly gets very messy.

Problem and Solution 40

COUNTING THE UNCOUNTABLE

(Problem Starter Sheet 40, page 136)
Suppose you are told that a heavy cloth bag contains some number of identical black marbles. If only one marble at a time can be removed, observed, and then returned to the bag, how can you find a good estimate of the number of marbles in the bag?

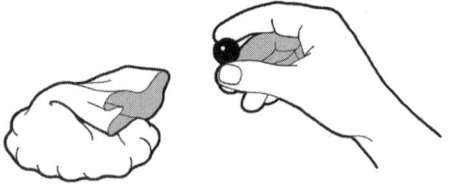

Understand the Problem
Facts
- There are some number of black marbles (n) in a bag.
- You cannot see through the bag because it is made of cloth.
- You can take out one marble at a time but must return it to the bag.

Condition
- You cannot mark the marbles in the bag when you view them one at a time.

Goal
- Find a good estimate of the number of marbles in the bag.

Select a Strategy
At first, this seems like an impossible problem to solve. Often when it appears there isn't enough information available to attempt a solution, you need to add a new element to the problem situation to provide insight into the unknown quantity—in this case the number of marbles in the bag.

Carry Out the Strategy
First, students can remove 1 marble and carefully observe its size, color, and weight. Then locate a new supply of marbles that are identical in every way except in color to the marbles in the bag (for example, 20 identical white marbles). Have them return the original black marble to the bag and thoroughly mix in the 20 white "seed" marbles with the other marbles in the bag. Draw 1 marble at a time, keeping track of the number of white (seed) and black (original)

marbles. The laws of probability tell us that the ratio of the number of seeded (white) marbles to the number of white marbles drawn is equal to the ratio of the number of original black marbles to the number of black marbles drawn.

$$\frac{\text{\# of seed marbles}}{\text{\# of seed marbles drawn}} = \frac{\text{original marbles}}{\text{\# original marbles drawn}}$$

The simplest way to estimate the number of original black marbles is to continue drawing marbles one at a time, replacing each and thoroughly mixing the marbles in the bag. Keep a systematic record of the white and black marbles drawn until 20 white marbles have been drawn; the number of black marbles drawn should equal the original number of black marbles in the bag. (Say that 30 black marbles were drawn in this case). The following proportion describes this result:

$$\begin{array}{c}\text{(white seed marbles)}\\ \text{(white marbles drawn)}\end{array}\frac{20}{20} = \frac{30}{30}\begin{array}{c}\text{(original marbles)}\\ \text{(black marbles drawn)}\end{array}$$

Students might also carry out an experiment of 100 trials (drawing and replacing one marble at a time and mixing the marbles thoroughly after each draw). Let's say they drew out a total of 40 white marbles and 60 black marbles, the number of original marbles (x) in the bag can be computed using the following proportion:

$$\frac{20}{40} = \frac{x}{60}$$

$$x = (20 \times 60) \div 40 = 30 \text{ original marbles}$$

Evaluate the Results
Comparing the number of white seed marbles drawn to the number of seed marbles added to the bag gives a ratio that is equal to the number of original black marbles drawn to the total number of black marbles originally in the bag. Increasing the number of white seed marbles or increasing the number of samples drawn can improve the predictive accuracy of this procedure. Because of the laws of probability, it is possible to select the same white or black marble more than once during the drawing process, but on the average the ratios remain equal if we thoroughly mix the marbles after each selection. This seeding procedure is used by wildlife management scientists to estimate the population of birds and fish in the wild and by medical professionals to aid in the diagnosis of disease.

Problem and Solution 41

SINGLE-STAIRCASE CONSTRUCTION

(Problem Starter Sheet 41, page 137)
How many blocks are needed to build a 20-step staircase that extends the 5 steps shown here?

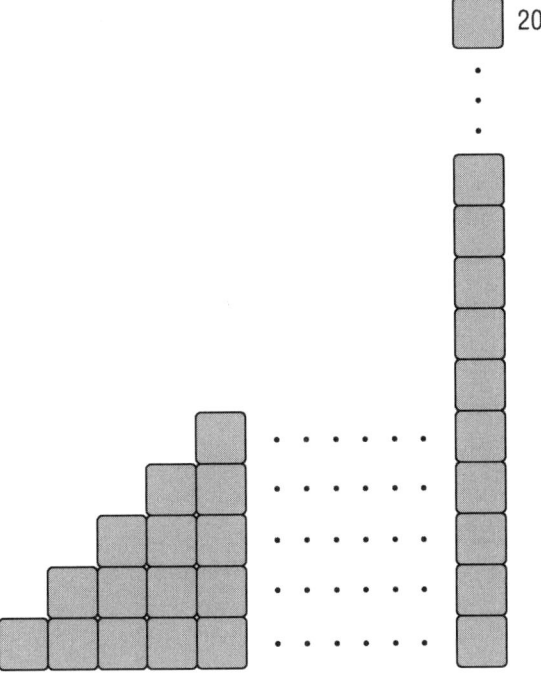

20 steps

Understand the Problem
Facts
- The staircase is constructed by stacking cubes in columns, each column one cube higher than the previous column.

Conditions
- All the cubes are the same size.
- The staircase is only one cube thick.

Goal
- Find the number of cubes needed for a 20-step staircase.

Select a Strategy
Instead of trying to count the blocks needed for a 20-step staircase, students can look at smaller staircases and see if they can find a pattern that helps them calculate the number of blocks needed for each staircase. They can then make a systematic list of the results.

Carry Out the Strategy
Have student start with the simplest 1-step staircase and build or draw a diagram of the first five staircases:

> 1 step needs 1 block
> 2 steps need 3 blocks
> 3 steps need 6 blocks
> 4 steps need 10 blocks
> 5 steps need 15 blocks

Point out that the total number of blocks required to construct the 4-step staircase equals the number of blocks needed to construct the 3-step staircase (6 blocks) plus the number of additional blocks needed to construct the fourth step (4 blocks). Five steps require the 4-step staircase, plus the number of blocks needed for the fifth step (10 + 5 = 15). As shown in the following table, we can continue the pattern to a 6-step staircase (5-step staircase + 6 blocks = 21 blocks), 7 steps (21 + 7 = 28), and so on up to the nineteenth step (171 + 19 = 190).

20-STEP STAIRCASE

# of Steps	# of Blocks
1	1
2	3
3	6
4	10
5	15
6	21
7	28
.	.
.	.
.	.
19	190
20	?

Evaluate the Results
Following the pattern in the table, we can compute the number of blocks needed to build the 20-step staircase. Adding the number of blocks needed for the twentieth step (20) to those required for the nineteenth staircase (190) gives a total of 210 blocks needed to build a 20-step staircase. Continue this pattern to calculate the number of blocks needed to build larger staircases.

Problem and Solution 42

DOUBLE-STAIRCASE CONSTRUCTION

(Problem Starter Sheet 42, page 138)

How many blocks are needed to construct a 10-step double staircase?

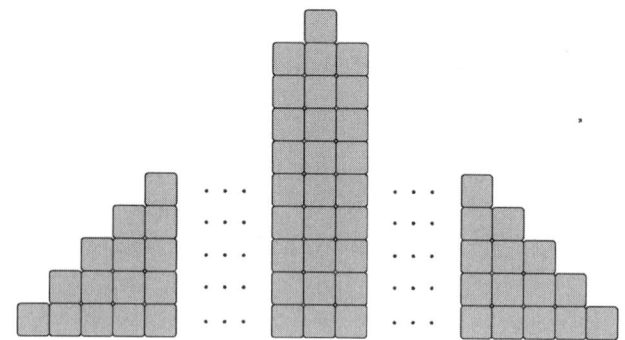

Understand the Problem

Facts

- A double staircase is constructed by stacking cubes in columns, each ascending and descending column one cube higher or lower than the previous column.
- A double staircase has the same number of ascending and descending steps.
- The height of the staircase is the number of steps required to reach the top.

Conditions

- All the cubes are the same size.
- The staircase is only one cube thick.

Goal

- Find the number of cubes needed for a 10-step double staircase.

Select a Strategy

Students can construct a simple staircase first, record the result in a table, and then build a larger staircase and search for a pattern that will help count the number of blocks required. They can use real cubes if they are available or draw a sketch using graph paper.

Carry Out the Strategy

A 1-step double staircase requires only one block. A 2-step double staircase requires four blocks. The following table shows the number of blocks required to build 1- through 5-step double staircases.

DOUBLE STAIRCASE

# of Steps	# of Blocks
1	1
2	4
3	9
4	?
5	?
6	?
.	.
.	.
.	.

To find the next value in the table, have students describe how the values in the second column increase. In the following table, the difference between each adjacent pair of values in column two follow the odd-number pattern (3, 5, 7, . . .). This pattern predicts that the next difference will be 9. The number of blocks in a 5-step double staircase is 25, so the difference between 16 and 25 is 9.

DOUBLE-STAIRCASE DIFFERENCE TABLE

# of Steps	# of Blocks Difference
1	1
	> 3
2	4
	> 5
3	9
	> 7
4	16
	> 9
5	25
	> 11
6	36
	>?
7	?
	>?
8	?
	>?
9	?
	>?
10	?

The number of blocks required for each successive step in a double staircase seems to grow according to this odd-number pattern. Given enough time, patience, and paper, this table could be extended to help calculate the number of blocks required for any double staircase.

Evaluate the Results

To calculate the number of blocks needed to construct a 10-step double staircase, continue the pattern to find the number needed for the 9-step staircase (81 blocks) and add the ninth odd number (19) to get the number of blocks needed to construct a 10-step double staircase (81 + 19 = 100). It is interesting to note the relationship of double-staircase construction to the single-staircase problem. Looking at the table in the previous problem, notice that combining two sequential single staircases creates a double staircase. For example, the figure below shows how to combine of a 4-step and 5-step single staircase to make a 5-step double staircase. Therefore, you can also use the single-staircase table to calculate the number of blocks needed for double staircases.

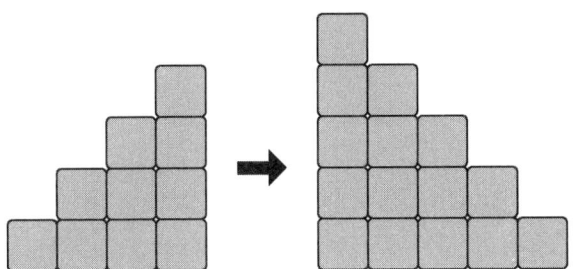

Problem and Solution 43

MUCH BIGGER DOUBLE-STAIRCASE CONSTRUCTION
(Problem Starter Sheet 43, page 139)
How many blocks are needed to construct a 100-step double staircase?

Understand the Problem

Facts
- In the 10-step double-staircase problem, we learned that the number of blocks needed grows by the odd-number sequence.
- Also, any double staircase is equivalent to two sequential single staircases.

Conditions
- All the cubes are the same size.
- The staircase is one block thick.
- Extending the 10-step double-staircase table to 100 steps will take too many blocks and too much time.

Goal
- Calculate the number of blocks needed to construct a 100-step double staircase.

Select a Strategy
Trying to extend the odd-number pattern from the previous problem would require that the number of blocks be computed for all the staircases in sequence to solve a larger problem. To use this method for a 100-step problem, students would have to calculate all the prior constructions up to and including 99 steps. This would take a lot of calculations and even more patience. To save time, have students try to develop a general rule (function) that directly relates the staircase height to the number of blocks required for construction.

Carry Out the Strategy
The following table lists the number of blocks needed to construct 1-step through 10-step double staircases. Instead of looking for a pattern that relates the values down the second column, ask students to look for a direct relationship between each number of steps in column one with its corresponding block count in column two.

DOUBLE STAIRCASES

# of Steps	# of Blocks
1	1
2	4
3	9
4	16
5	25
6	36
7	49
8	64
9	81
10	100

To help visualize this relationship, look at the shape resulting from reorganizing a double staircase that is shown below.

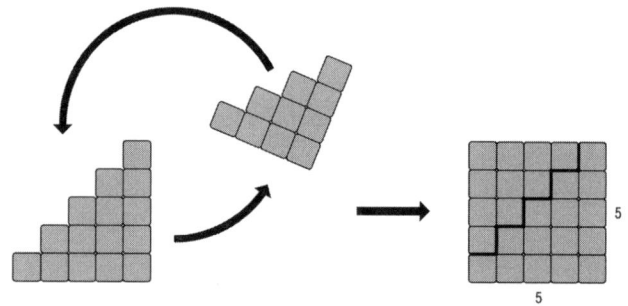

The total number of blocks can be easily computed by multiplying the staircase height by itself ($4 \times 4 = 16$ blocks). A 100-step double staircase will require $100 \times 100 = 10,000$ blocks.

Evaluate the Results
By multiplying the step number by itself, we can quickly calculate the number of blocks needed for double staircases. The sequence of values in the second column of the following table is called the square numbers. A square number results from multiplying any whole number by itself ($n \times n = n^2$). The physical pattern of flipping the descending stairs on top of the ascending stairs should continue to create squares for larger and larger double staircases. It seems reasonable that this rule will continue to work for larger staircases. You might want to test a few more examples to be sure. There is a real advantage to creating a general rule, or mathematical function, that relates each value in the first column in a table to its corresponding value in the second column in this case $100^2 = 10,000$. If we had to rely

on continuing a pattern to find the solution much further down the table, it would first be necessary compute all the intervening answers. Knowing the function that relates column one entries to each corresponding value in column two allows you to skip all the intermediary steps and calculate the answer immediately. For example, the number of blocks necessary to construct a 1,000-step double staircase is $10,002 = 1,000,000$.

Section III

Reproducible
Problem Starters

Problem Starter 1

Name: ....

Date: ....

FIND THAT HOMEWORK

Before excusing the class, the teacher said that their assignment that night was to "find" their homework. She said that the homework assignment was on two facing pages in their textbook, and the sum of the two page numbers equaled 65. What homework pages were assigned?

What are the homework pages if the two-page total equals 100?

_____

What are the homework pages if three pages are assigned and the total is 135?

_____

 *Hint:* Look at a textbook and notice where odd and even pages appear in the book.

Problem Starter 2

Name:

Date:

TOOTH TRUTHS

Which grade level in your school is missing the most teeth?

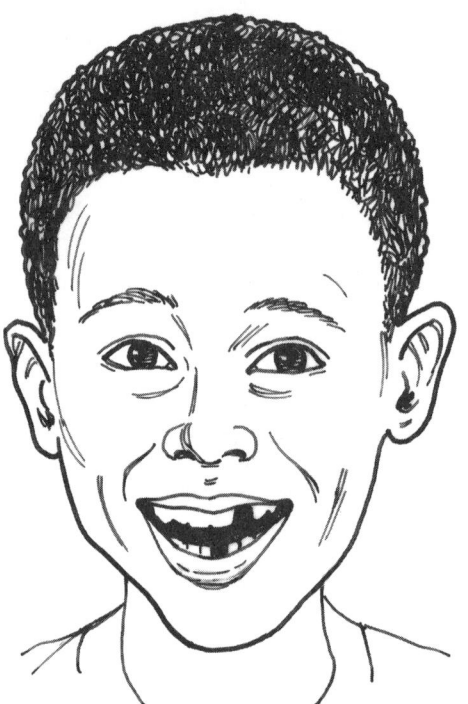

 *Hint:* Fill in the table to help you find out:

TEACHER	GRADE	MISSING TEETH

Problem Starter 3   Name:

                                                         Date:

FRUIT FACTS

Oranges are a famous fruit first found in China. They come in many sizes and colors. Some have thick skins, some thin. Some are sweet while others are bitter. Do all oranges have the same number of sections? How many seeds are in an orange? Does it matter if they are big or small? See if you can find out.

 *Hint:* Next time you're at the grocery store, talk with the grocer about the different types of oranges. Peel one and count the seeds and sections. Write your answers on the following table and compare them with your friend's.

SEEDS	SECTIONS

Problem Starter 4

Name:

Date:

MYSTERY MASSES

You need:

and:

Put the boxes in order from lightest to heaviest. Write the mystery word the boxes spell:

Light

Heavy

  *Hint:* Use the to help you compare the mystery masses.

Problem Starter 5

Name: ....

Date: ....

APPLE SHARING
You need:

You

Two friends

One apple

Share an apple so that you and your two friends get the same amount.

How many seeds are in the apple? _____

Do all apples have the same number of seeds? _____

TYPE OF APPLE	NUMBER OF SEEDS
1. Red Delicious	9
2.	
3.	
4.	

Put the seeds in the sun for a few days to dry them out. Plant them and see what happens.

Hint: Take turns cutting the apple. The last person to cut chooses last. Go to the supermarket and talk to the grocer about apples.

Problem Starter 6   Name: ....

                          Date: ....

CLAY BOATS

You need:

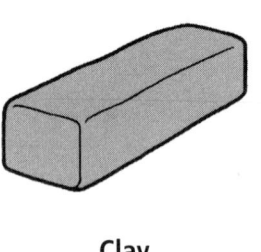

Clay

Pail of water

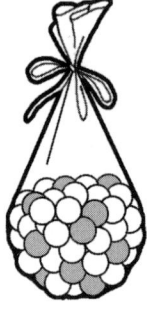

Marbles

Can you make a clay boat that floats?

Try it.

See how many marbles it will carry.

Hint: Pinch the walls very thin and plug any holes.

Problem Starter 7   Name:

                                               Date:

COOL COSTS

It takes more gas to run a car with the air conditioner turned on than with it off. (If you open the windows when the air conditioner is off, however, there may not be much difference in the mileage due to the wind resistance caused by the open windows.) The table below shows the miles per gallon of gasoline for a car with and without the air conditioner running.

MILEAGE WITH AND WITHOUT AIR CONDITIONING (A/C)

	Speed in MPH				
	40	**45**	**50**	**55**	**60**
Without air conditioning	34	33	31	29	26
With air conditioning	32	31	28	26	22

How much extra will it cost to run the air conditioner for a 4-hour, 45-minute trip at 55 miles per hour if gasoline costs $2.09 per gallon?

_____

Hint: Try using simpler numbers (like $2.00 instead of $2.09) to more easily work out the calculations needed, and then substitute the actual numbers to find the final answer.

Problem Starter 8

Name: _____

Date: _____

CHANGING CHANGE

How many ways could you make 16¢?

You need:

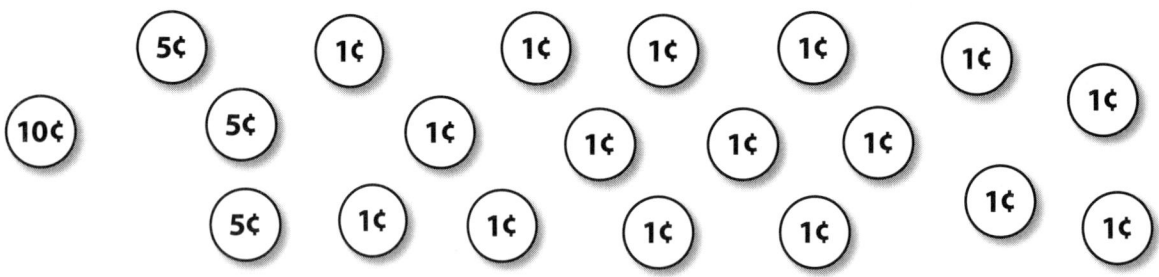

CHANGE FOR 16¢

	10¢	5¢	1¢	
1	1 dime	1 nickel	1 penny	=16¢
2				=16¢
3				=16¢
4				=16¢
5				=16¢
6				=16¢

 *Hint:* Fill in the table above. Count the different ways to make 16¢.

Problem Starter 9   Name:

                                                        Date:

CANDY BARS

Here are some whole candy bars:

Here are some candy bars with bites out of them:

No candy bar can have more than 9 units on an edge:

How many different candy bars with no bites can you make?

Hint: Using grid paper, cut out as many different whole candy bars as you can.

Remember: is the same as:

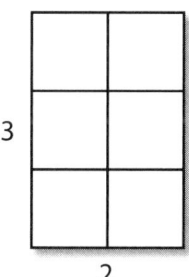   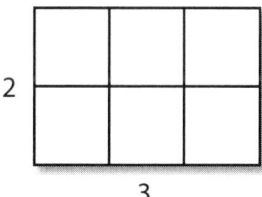

Problem Starter 10

Name:

Date:

CLASS ALLOWANCE

How much money does your class spend in a year? If you need to, use a calculator to find the totals.

 *Hint:* Fill in the table below.

CLASS INCOME FOR ONE WEEK

Student	Allowance	Lunch and Milk Money	Total		Student	Allowance	Lunch and Milk Money	Total
1					17			
2					18			
3					19			
4					20			
5					21			
6					22			
7					23			
8					24			
9					25			
10					26			
11					27			
12					28			
13					29			
14					30			
15					31			
16					32			

Total for one week

Total for one year (× 52)

Problem Starter 11

Name:

Date:

PENCIL SURVIVAL

How long does a pencil last in your class? To find out you will need:

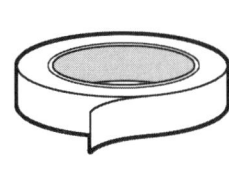

Hint: Before using a new pencil, put a small piece of tape around the top.
Write the date it is first sharpened. When it is used up, fill in the table below:

PENCIL LIFE SPAN

	Date First Sharpened	Date Used Up	Number of School Days Used
1			
2			
3			
4			
5			
6			
7			
8			
9			
10			
		Total	

Use a calculator to find the average. Divide the total days by the number of pencils. Average: _____

Problem Starter 12

Name:

Date:

PAINTING NUMBERS

A town decided to paint house numbers on the mailbox in front of each home to make it easier for the post office to deliver mail. The houses were numbered in sequence (1, 2, 3, 4, . . .). It cost $1 to paint each digit on the mailboxes. The Town Council determined it needed to budget exactly $600 for the job. How many houses were there in the town?

How many houses would there be in another town if that town's council had to budget $2,893 to paint its house numbers? _____

 *Hint:* Try splitting the problem into smaller parts and recording the results in a table.

Problem Starter 13

Name:

Date:

T.V. HOURS

How much television do you watch in one year?
If you need to, use a calculator.

Hint: Try splitting the problem into smaller parts and recording the results in a table.

DAY	T.V. HOURS
Monday	
Tuesday	
Wednesday	
Thursday	
Friday	
Saturday	
Sunday	
Total for Week	
Total for Year (× 52)	

Problem Starter 14

Name:

Date:

HOT LUNCH

Which school lunch does your class like best? To find out, you need:

SCHOOL LUNCH MENU

Mon	Tues	Wed	Thur	Fri

MENU

Week	Monday	Tuesday	Wednesday	Thursday	Friday
1	Menu _____ Buy_____ Bring _____ **Total** _____	Menu _____ Buy _____ Bring_____ **Total**_____	Menu _____ Buy _____ Bring_____ **Total**_____	Menu _____ Buy _____ Bring_____ **Total**_____	Menu _____ Buy _____ Bring_____ **Total**_____
2	Menu _____ Buy_____ Bring _____ **Total** _____	Menu _____ Buy _____ Bring_____ **Total**_____	Menu _____ Buy _____ Bring_____ **Total**_____	Menu _____ Buy _____ Bring_____ **Total**_____	Menu _____ Buy _____ Bring_____ **Total**_____
3	Menu _____ Buy_____ Bring _____ **Total** _____	Menu _____ Buy _____ Bring_____ **Total**_____	Menu _____ Buy _____ Bring_____ **Total**_____	Menu _____ Buy _____ Bring_____ **Total**_____	Menu _____ Buy _____ Bring_____ **Total**_____
4	Menu _____ Buy_____ Bring _____ **Total** _____	Menu _____ Buy _____ Bring_____ **Total**_____	Menu _____ Buy _____ Bring_____ **Total**_____	Menu _____ Buy _____ Bring_____ **Total**_____	Menu _____ Buy _____ Bring_____ **Total**_____

Hint: Fill in the table with the number of buyers and brownbaggers. Use your calculator to help you find which foods are the most popular.

Problem Starter 15　　　　　　　　Name:

Date:

FOLDING BOXES
Which of these twelve figures will fold into an open-end box?
Fold only on dotted lines.

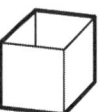

1　　　　　　2　　　　　　3　　　　　　4

5　　　　　　6　　　　　　7　　　　　　8

9　　　　　10　　　　　11　　　　12

Hint: Cut out these figures and try to fold them into a box. You might also try cutting off the
top of several small milk cartons and see which of the above shapes you can make by cutting
along the edges. Remember, the figure must be in one piece.

Name:

Date:

WHAT'S IN A SHADOW?

If the shadow of a 6-foot-tall man is 4 feet long, how tall is a tree that casts a 10-foot shadow?

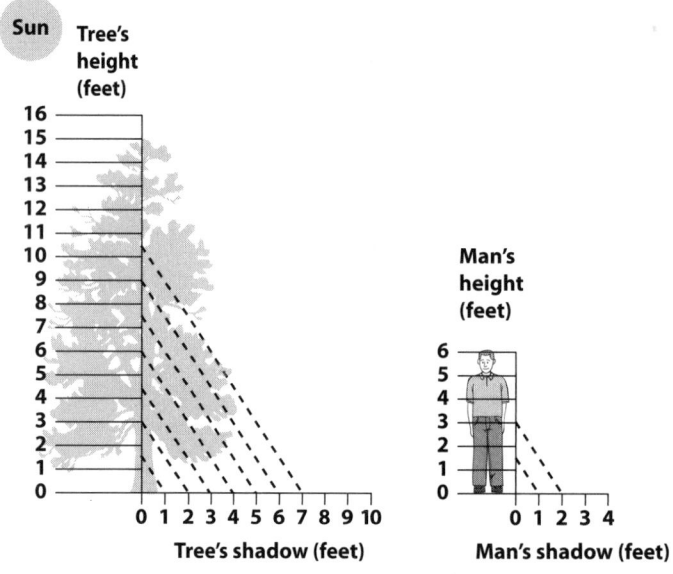

 *Hint:* A 10-foot pole casts a shadow twice as long as a 5-foot pole. The heights of the poles are proportional to their shadow lengths. Try using graph paper and making a scale drawing of the man, the tree, and their shadows.

Problem Starter 17

Name: ....

Date: ....

WHAT'S THE DIFFERENCE?

1. Pick any four numbers and write them in a square, as below.

$$4 \qquad 8$$

$$7 \qquad 1$$

2. Next, connect any two numbers without going across the middle. Find the difference between the two number values and write it at the center of the line.

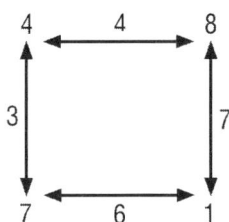

3. Connect the anwsers with arrows as in the following figure and find the diffence again.

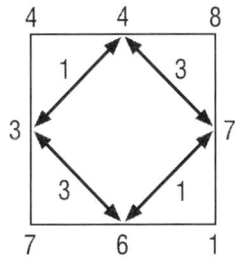

4. Now connect these anwsers with lines and find their differences again.

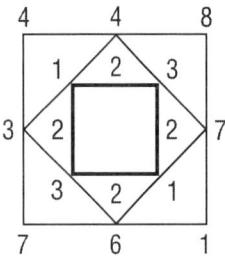

This time all the answers are the same (2).

Will this always happen for any four starting numbers?

Will you always end up with 2 for a final answer?

What happens if you start with bigger numbers?

This problem needed three steps to get to a common difference. Can you find four numbers that need four steps? Five steps? Six steps? Seven Steps?

Hint: Try many combinations of four numbers. Keep a record of the original four numbers, the number of differences, and the final answer.

Problem Starter 18   Name:

                                          Date:

GOLD DIGGERS

Digger Jenkins was a gold assayer who flew all over Alaska in a rickety little plane weighing ore for eager prospectors. His job was to weigh samples very accurately, but he also had to be careful not to overload his tiny plane with equipment. To measure weight, he packed only a balance and three mass pieces—1-gram, 3-gram, and 9-gram weights. For example, he could weigh a 4-gram sample of gold ore like this:

Ore–4 grams   1 gram + 3 grams

Digger claimed he could weigh any amount of ore from 1 to 13 grams. (No fractions, of course.) Is Digger right?

 *Hint:* Find a pan balance and the 1-, 3-, and 9-gram mass pieces, conduct several experiments, and organize the results in a table. Remember, the mass pieces can go on either pan.

From *Solving Math Problems Kids Care About.* Copyright © 2006 Good Year Books.

Problem Starter 19

Name:

Date:

THE GREAT DIVIDE

Otto Levique and his family were taking a trip across Canada by car. When they came to the Rocky Mountains, his daughter, Michelle, who had been studying geography in school, explained that they would soon cross the Great Divide—an imaginary line running lengthwise along the highest points of a mountain range. Rain falling to the east of this line ends up in the Atlantic Ocean, and to the west in the Pacific Ocean. It was an exciting moment when they crossed the "roof of the continent," but they were all surprised when they crossed the imaginary line more than once. Look at the map to see how this could happen.

Michelle kept a record of the number of times they crossed the Great Divide. She thought it was odd that they crossed the line five times on their route from Edmonton to Vancouver and seven times on their return, making a total of twelve crossings for the round trip. Will every round trip through the mountains always have an even number of Great Divide crossings? Help the Leviques with their auto-dilemma.

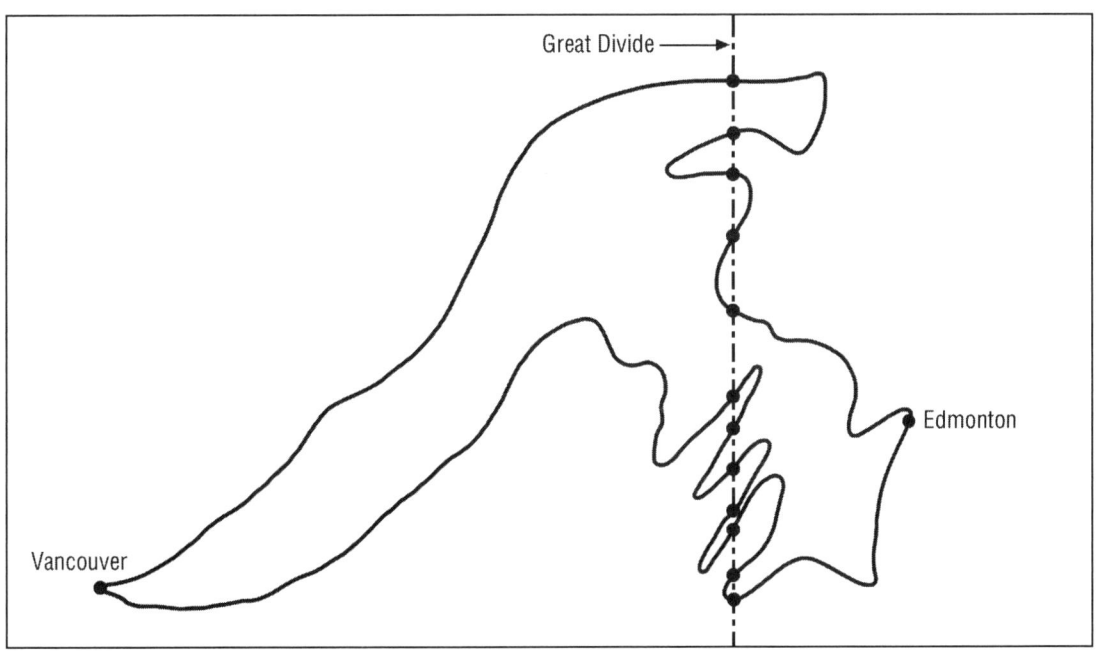

 *Hint:* Draw a map of an imaginary Great Divide. Do several experiments, organize the results in a table, and look for patterns.

Problem Starter 20

Name:

Date:

MAKING A RACE FAIR

A turtle and a rabbit ran a 1,000-meter race. The turtle ran 10 meters each minute and the rabbit ran 100 meters each minute. The turtle was also given a 500-meter head start. Who won the race? Was it a fair race?

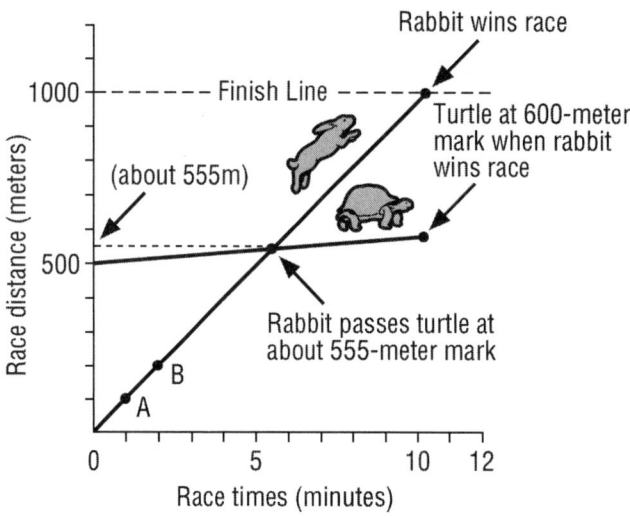

How much of a head start would the turtle need for the race to be fair?

 *Hint:* Try constructing a graph with the racetrack distance along the vertical axis and the race time along the horizontal. Draw lines that track the progress of the turtle and rabbit from beginning of the race to the end.

Problem Starter 21

Name: ....

Date: ....

STACK THE DECK

Here is an interesting card trick to try with your friends. Write each letter of your name on separate, identical cards. Form them into a deck with the faces down and shuffle the deck. Slip the top card under the deck, still facedown. Deal the second card faceup on the table. Slip the third card under the deck and deal the next card faceup next to the first. Continue this process until all the cards form a line on the table.

You would be lucky indeed if the cards spelled a word. However, can you find a way to stack the deck so that when you deal out the cards as above, it spells your name?

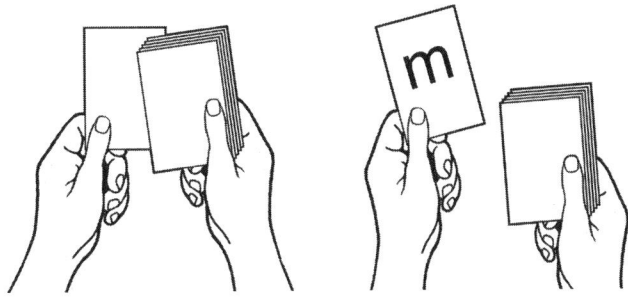

Slip one card under deck. Deal next card faceup.

If you can figure out a solution, it's fun to surprise a friend by a using a deck of cards that spells out his or her name.

Hint: Try starting with your name spelled on the table and follow the steps backward to arrange the deck.

Problem Starter 22   Name:

                                                Date:

FOUR ACES

This simple card trick sounds complicated but it is actually very easy to do.

1. Using an ordinary deck of cards, cut the cards into four roughly equal piles and lay them out next to each other in front of you.
2. Pick up the pile that came from the bottom of the deck (pile 4), and deal three cards facedown on the table in the same spot where the pile was.
3. Deal one card from pile 4 facedown on top of each of the other three decks and place the pile back where it came from, on top of the three cards.
4. Repeat the process with the other three piles, ending with the pile that was on top of the original deck (pile 1).
5. Turning over the top card on each pile gives a surprising results—four aces!

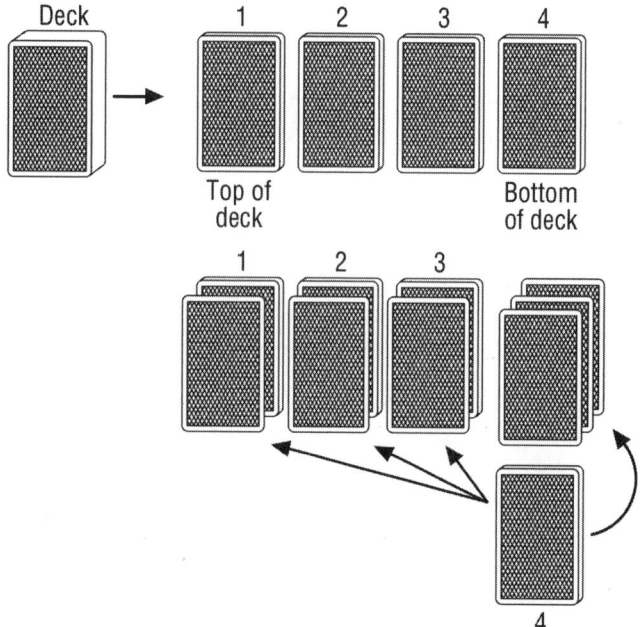

- Pick up pile 4
- Deal 3 cards facedown
- Deal 1 card on piles 1, 2, and 3
- Replace pile 4
- Repeat the process with 1, 2, and 3

Can you figure out how the trick works?

 *Hint:* Work the problem backward and see how to initially stack the deck with the four aces to allow the trick to work.

From Solving Math Problems Kids Care About. Copyright © 2006 Good Year Books.

Problem Starter 23

Name: ....

Date: ....

STACK 'EM HIGH

Suzanne Megapenny is very rich. She got a bit bored one day and told her banker to immediately deliver one million new one-dollar bills to her house. She sat in her living room and began to stack the bills on top of each other in a single column. How high will the stack be?

Hint: Find how many dollars (pieces of paper) it takes to make a pile 1 centimeter thick. Use your calculator to find out the height of a million dollars.

Problem Starter 24   Name:

                                                         Date:

COUNT ON

One rainy afternoon Tara couldn't find anyone to play with, so she decided to count to a billion. Can you find out how long it would take Tara to finish? One hour? Two hours? All day?

How old are you in seconds?

Hint: Figure it takes about one second to say one number and use your calculator to help you crunch the big numbers.

Problem Starter 25

Name:

Date:

GRAINS OF RICE

How many grains of rice are in a bag of rice? One hundred grains? One thousand grains? One million grains? To find out, you need:

A bag of rice

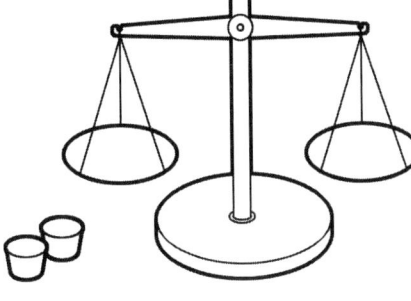

A pan-balance scale

A calculator

Hint: Measure out one small cup of rice. Count the grains in the cup.
Use the pan balance and calculator to help find the total number of grains in the bag.

Problem Starter 26

Name:

Date:

MONEY MATTERS

One day, Rosa decided to play a trick on her brother, Aaron. She said, "I have 21¢ in my pocket. If you can tell me all the possible combinations of pennies, nickels, and dimes that make up 21¢, I'll buy you an ice cream cone. Here is one way.

$$\boxed{10¢} \quad \boxed{5¢} \quad \boxed{5¢} \quad \boxed{1¢} \quad = \quad 21¢$$

After Aaron started making his list, Rosa said, "I just found a silver dollar in my other pocket. If you can find all the ways to make change for $1.21, I'll buy you a double-dipper cone. You can use pennies, nickels, dimes, quarters, half dollars, and a silver dollar. Here is one way:

$$\boxed{\$1} \quad \boxed{10¢} \quad \boxed{10¢} \quad \boxed{1¢} = \$1.21$$

Hint: Make a list of all the ways to make change for 21¢ and $1.21.
Try to follow a regular pattern so you don't skip any answers.

From *Solving Math Problems Kids Care About.* Copyright © 2006 Good Year Books.

Problem Starter 27

Name: _____

Date: _____

ICE-CREAM EXPERT

Bud was an expert ice-cream eater. He could name any flavor blindfolded. When he bought an ice-cream cone, not only did he choose the flavors carefully, but he had to have them stacked on the cone in the right order. Strawberry on top with vanilla on the bottom was for hot days. Vanilla on top and strawberry on the bottom helped him to think better.

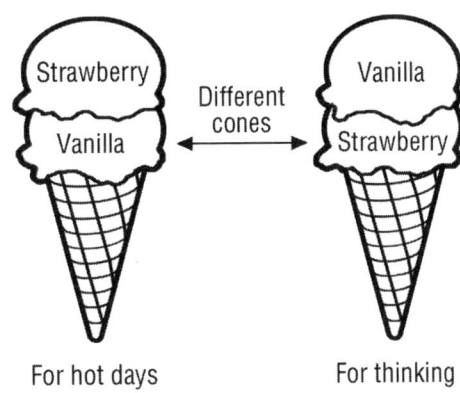

There are only two ways of building a cone with two flavors. (You must use both flavors.) How many different cones could Bud order with three flavors? Four flavors? Five flavors?

Hint: Make a list of all possible cones. Start with one flavor, then two and so on. Try to follow a pattern so you won't skip any. Using different-colored blocks as flavors may help you keep track of the different cones.

Problem Starter 28

Name:

Date:

WHO'S SHAKING WHOSE?

If ten people are attending a meeting, how many handshakes are required for each person to greet every other person exactly once?

 *Hint:* Try to break the problem into parts and systematically list the results in a table. Remember if Shannon shakes Cooper's hand and later Cooper shakes Shannon's hand, we do not count it as a new handshake.

Problem Starter 29

Name:

Date:

HAMBURGER HEAVEN

Here is the menu for the local hamburger hangout.

HAMBURGER HEAVEN		
Burgers	**Fries 'n' Rings**	**Drinks**
1. Boring Burger.. 30¢	1. French Fries ......45¢	1. Orange ....38¢
2. Kiloburger .... 75¢	2. Onion Rings......65¢	2. Cola ....30¢
3. Fat Burger $1.50		3. Root Beer..........30¢
		4. Milk....................55¢

If you could pick one item from each column, how many different meals could you make? Here are two different meals:

1. Fat Burger, Onion Rings, Root Beer
2. Fat Burger, French Fries, Milk

How many meals would be possible if a veggie burger was added to the menu?

 *Hint:* Make a list of meals. Try to follow a regular pattern so you won't miss any combinations.

Problem Starter 30

Name:

Date:

POPCORN TRUTH

Companies are always advertising that their product is better than the rest. "Our toothpaste makes your teeth whiter," or "Kids eat more Corn Puffies than any other cereal." Ever wonder if the commercials are true? Here is an ad for you to test out for yourself.

You pay a little more, but our popcorn leaves fewer unpopped kernels, so it's a better buy.

Go to the store and buy the same-sized bag of the most expensive and least expensive popcorn. Do an experiment to find out if the expensive popcorn is actually a better buy.

Hint: Pop equal amounts and compare the results to the purchase price. Use a calculator to help with the arithmetic.

Problem Starter 31

Name:

Date:

COW THOUGHTS

Pico Steerman, a well-known rancher, invented a new style of corral for his cattle. By driving a herd of steers through gate *A*, the cow-doctor could check them one a time for disease at Exit *B*.

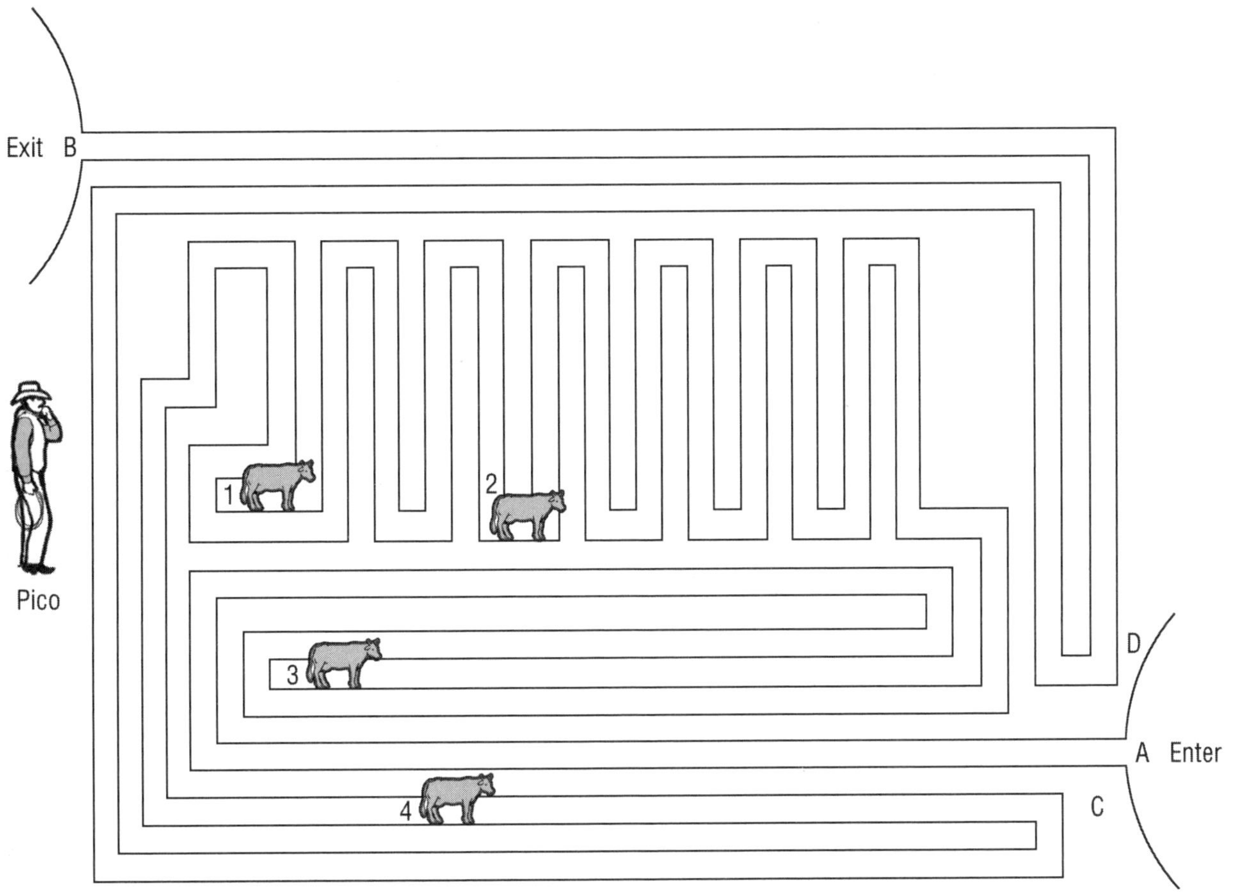

Hint: Try making a very simple corral that looks like an ordinary circle and figure out a simple way to show that a cow is inside. Think about what must be true for a cow to be really trapped. If you're outside, how many fences are between you and the cow? Make the corral more and more complicated, keep a record of your results and look for patterns. Do the same experiment with the cow outside the corral. Compare the inside and outside results.

Problem Starter 32

Name:

Date:

CLASSROOM MANEUVERS

Mr. Nitpicker's classroom is organized in five neat rows with five desks in each row. The desks are separated so you can walk in front and behind, as well as between them.

Arthur and the teacher are standing as in the picture. What is the shortest route for Arthur to walk in order to ask Mr. Nitpicker for a hall pass? Here are two possible routes:

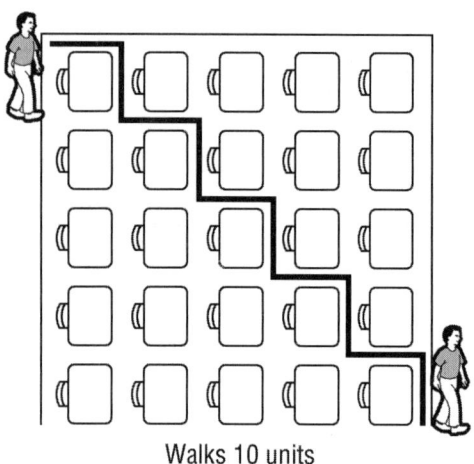

Walks 10 units

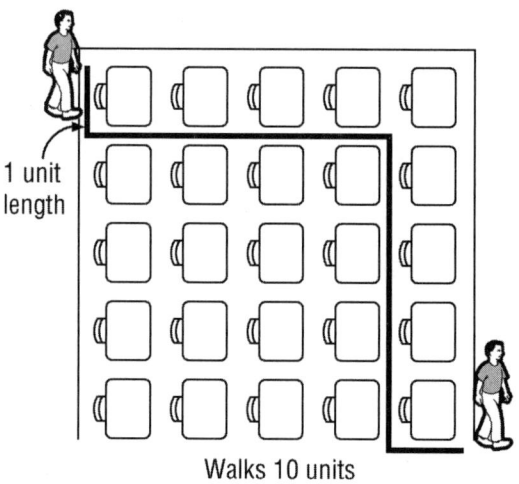

1 unit length

Walks 10 units

Hint: Find some squared paper and mark off several five-unit squares. Using this simple sketch (model), trace several routes and count the number of units Arthur has to walk.

Problem Starter 33

Name:

Date:

THE PURLOINED SAPPHIRE

Inspector Chang was called in to investigate the case of the missing sapphire. The gem was the centerpiece of a beautiful fountain in the middle of a courtyard. There were four rooms opening onto the courtyard, so one of four people staying in these rooms must have been responsible. But which one?

The only clue was the track of footprints left by the thief when he got his or her feet wet removing the sapphire. The thief left the path below, hoping to confuse the investigation. Chang took one look at the trail and immediately pointed at the person in room C as the culprit. How did she know for sure?

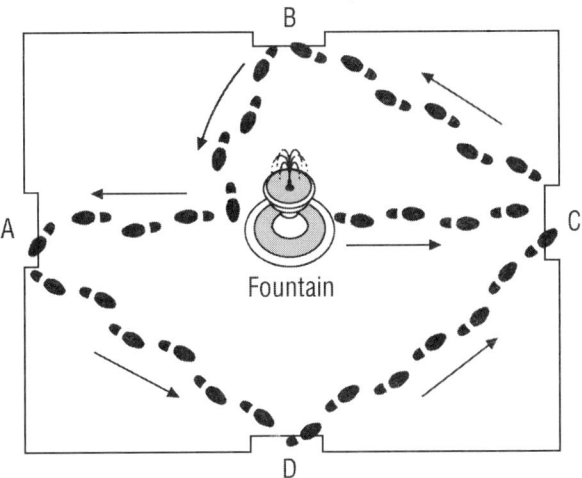

Fountain

 *Hint:* Make a simple sketch of the culprit's path and try tracing it without lifting your pencil or going over a line twice. Design other simple networks like those below and see if they can be traced without lifting your pencil or going over a line twice. Keep a table and look for a pattern.

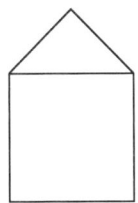 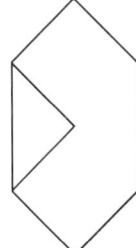 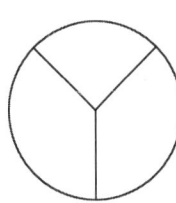 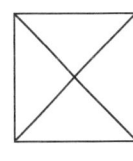

Problem Starter 34   Name:

                                                          Date:

LINE'ARDO DAVINCI

Line'ardo paints the white line down the middle of the road in his country. He is trying to conserve fuel, so he checks out his map each morning to plan his shortest route. Can Line'ardo "line" all the roads connecting the four cities below without retracing any routes? If so, where should he start?

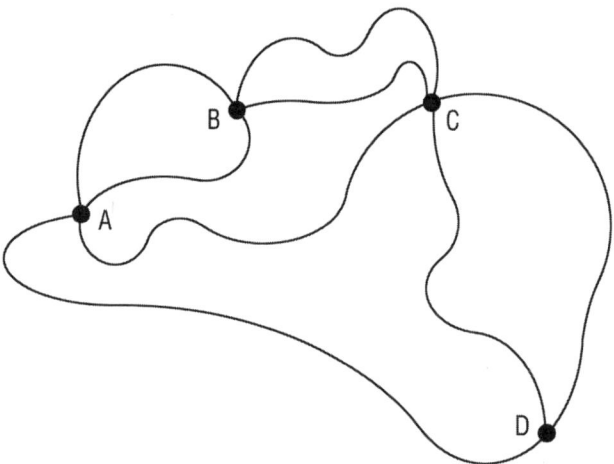

From *Solving Math Problems Kids Care About*. Copyright © 2006 Good Year Books.

 *Hint:* Make a simple sketch of the map above using as many straight lines as possible. Try tracing the figure without lifting your pencil or retracing any routes. It may be helpful to experiment first with very simple figures, record the results, and look for patterns.

Problem Starter 35

Name:

Date:

JAILHOUSE BLUES

The locks on prison doors work like this:

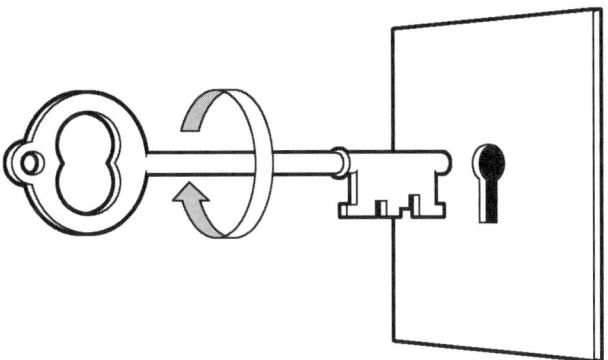

First turn—open
Second turn—closed
Third turn—open
Fourth turn—closed
And so on . . .

One night when the prisoners were sleeping, he quietly turned all the locks once, opening all the cells. He began to worry that he may have freed too many prisoners so he went back and turned every second lock (2, 4, 6, 8, . . . 24), which locked half the cells. Thinking that there still might be too many prisoners freed, he gave every third lock a turn (3, 6, 9, 12, . . . 24), then every fourth lock (4, 8, 12, . . . 24), fifth (5, 10, 15, 20, 25), sixth (6, 12, 18, 24), seventh, eighth, ninth, tenth, eleventh, and so on all the way to the every twenty-fifth (of course, he only turned one lock for every thirteenth and above).

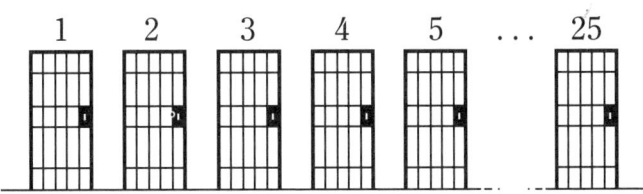

Who got out of jail in the morning?

Hint: Make a list of cells numbered 1 to 25. Keep track of the turns for each; look for a pattern.

Problem Starter 36

Name:

Date:

BILL YUD POOL

Bill Yud was an avid pool player. He enjoyed impressing his friends with his feats of pool table skill. He invented a new pool table that could be adjusted to almost any size and had pockets in only three of the four corners. Someone would call out any size table and old Bill would think for a minute and then point to one of the pockets. Next he would place the ball in the lower-left corner and shoot out at a 45° angle. That ball would scoot all over the table and sure enough would fall into the chosen pocket. He never missed! Can you figure out what Bill was up to? Here are a few examples.

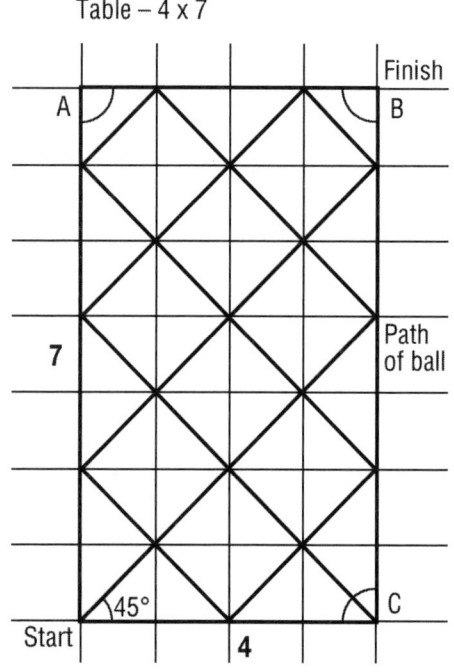

 *Hint:* Find some 1-cm graph paper and play several games on different-sized "Bill Yud" tables. Organize the data in a table and look for patterns.

Problem Starter 37   Name:

                                           Date:

FARMING A FIELD

A farmer needs to know how much area his fields cover so he can buy the correct amount of seed and fertilizer. Aggie McDonald's farm has trees planted in a regular square pattern. Aggie's grandfather planted the trees years ago to help him compute the area of various-shaped fields for planting.

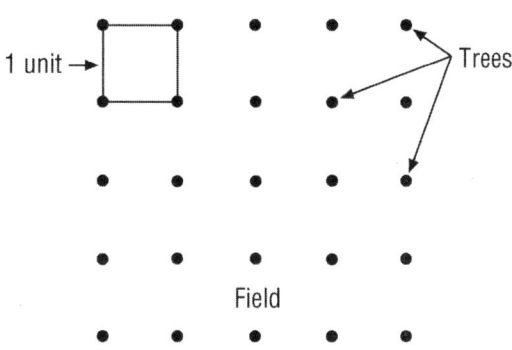

Aggie liked to plant interesting shaped fields of corn, beans, and squash. (Rectangular fields can be a bit boring to plow.) Can you use the tree pattern to help Aggie figure out these areas in unit squares? (A "unit" is the area of the small squares formed by the tree pattern.)

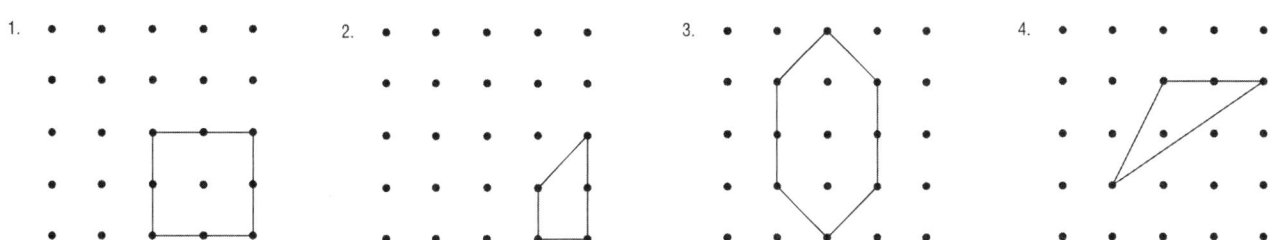

Try some other shapes. Can you find the area of any shaped field? (Make sure the corners lie on a tree; only straight edges, please.)

Hint: You might try using a geoboard to help "field" these problems.

Problem Starter 38

Name:

Date:

CLYDE THE CLASS CLOWN

One day Clyde got caught putting a toad in Mrs. Purdy's purse. For days, he didn't get called on to take the lunch count to the office. He spent the whole weekend trying to figure out a solution for his problem. Early Monday morning he asked Mrs. Purdy if she would pick the class messenger in the following way:

After attendance, everyone sits in a circle with the teacher in the center. Each students counts off one at a time (1, 2, 3, 4, . . .). Once everyone has a number, the teacher begins sending children to the their seats by skipping number 1, sending number 2, skipping number 3, sending number 4 and so on until she goes around the circle completely. She doesn't stop, however, and continues skipping every other student until only one is left. This lucky person gets to take the lunch count to the office. If there are ten students in the class, lucky number 5 will be chosen.

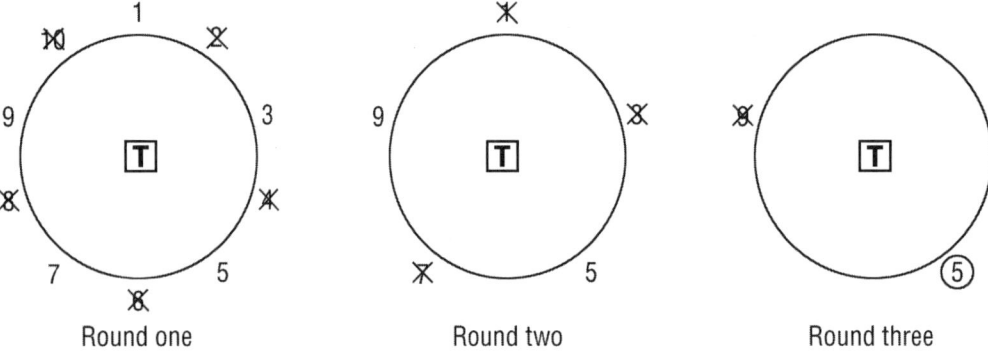

Round one   Round two   Round three

Where should Clyde sit if there are eleven students? Twelve students? Fifteen students? Twenty students? Twenty-five students? Thirty students? Can you find a rule that works for any size class?

 *Hint:* Make sketches of different-sized class circles and organize the results in a table. Look for patterns.

Problem Starter 39   Name:

Date:

THE BICYCLE DILEMMA

Cary rode her bicycle to the pet store after school every day to help clean the bird cages. There was only one bike rack near the store and Cary noticed it was full about half the time. She tried to convince the shop owner to put in one more rack so she wouldn't have to worry about losing her bike while she was working.

With one bike rack Cary can lock up her bike when she works four out of eight days. On the average, how many out of every eight working days should she find a parking space if a second rack were installed?

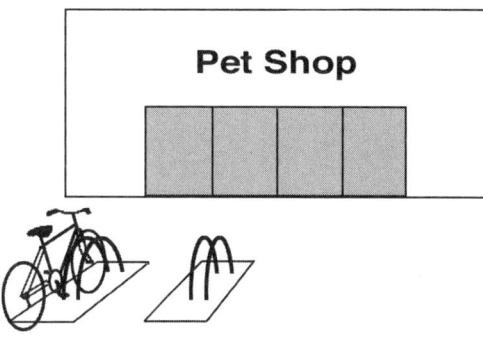

 *Hint:* The problem is similar to flipping one or two coins for one or two bike racks. Let heads represent a full rack, and tails an empty one. Flip one coin and keep a record of heads and tails in a table. Do the same with two coins. Look for a pattern.

Problem Starter 40   Name:

                                                            Date:

COUNTING THE UNCOUNTABLE

Suppose you are told that a heavy cloth bag contains some number of identical black marbles. If only one marble at a time can be removed, observed, and then returned to the bag, how can you find a good estimate of the number of marbles in the bag?

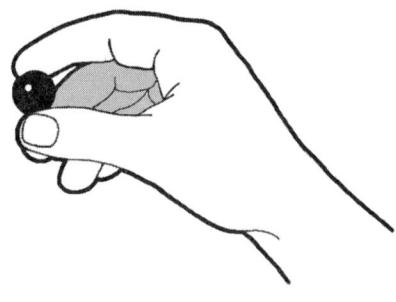

Hint: Often when it appears there isn't enough information available to solve a problem, you need to add a new element to the problem situation. First, remove 1 marble and carefully observe its size, color, and weight. Then find 20 marbles of the same size but a different color and add them to the bag. Now see if you can do an experiment and keep a careful record of the number of marbles of each color to help you figure out how many marbles were in the bag originally.

Problem Starter 41

Name:

Date:

SINGLE-STAIRCASE CONSTRUCTION

How many blocks are needed to build a 20-step staircase that completes the 5 steps shown here?

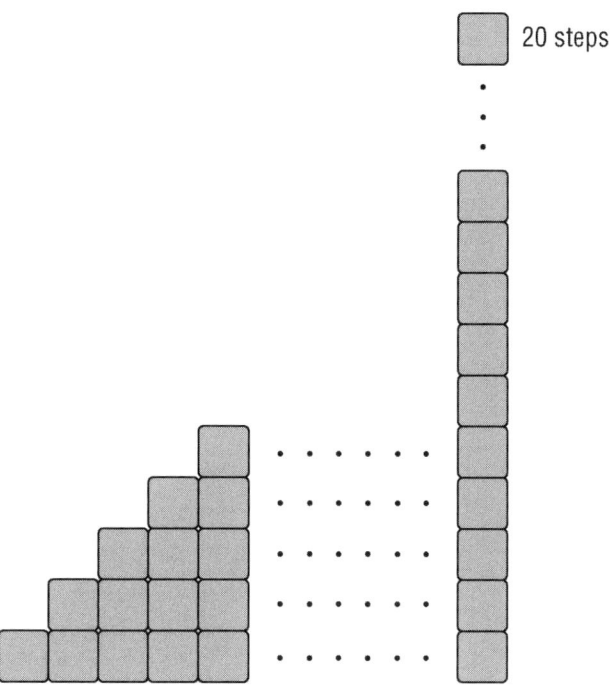

20 steps

 *Hint:* Start with the simplest staircase, build or draw sketches of larger staircases, and systematically record your results in a table. Look for a pattern in the table that helps you to figure out how many blocks are needed for the 20-step staircase.

Problem Starter 42

Name:

Date:

DOUBLE-STAIRCASE CONSTRUCTION

How many blocks are needed to construct a 10-step double staircase?

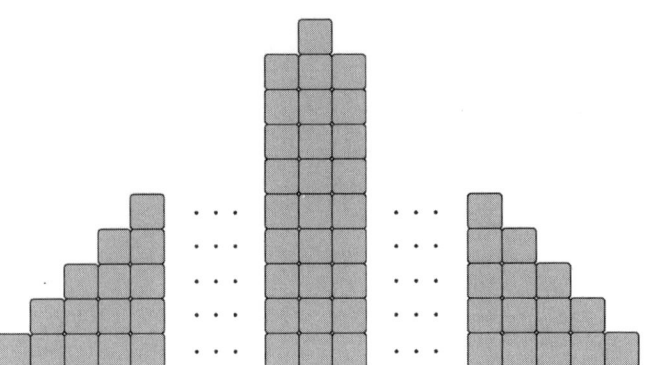

 *Hint:* Start with the simplest staircase, build or draw sketches of larger double staircases, and systematically record your results in a table like the one below. Complete the table below and look for a pattern that helps you to figure out how many blocks are needed for the 10-step double staircase.

DOUBLE STAIRCASE

# of Steps	# of Blocks
1	1
2	4
3	9
4	?
5	?
6	?
.	.
.	.
.	.

Problem Starter 43

Name:

Date:

MUCH BIGGER DOUBLE-STAIRCASE CONSTRUCTION

How many blocks are needed to construct a 100-step double staircase? Here is the table showing the number of blocks needed for the double staircases from steps 1 to 10:

DOUBLE STAIRCASES

# of Steps	# of Blocks
1	1
2	4
3	9
4	16
5	25
6	36
7	49
8	64
9	81
10	100
⋮	⋮
100	?

Hint: Trying to use the odd-number pattern from the previous problem to find the number of blocks in a 100-step double staircase would require knowing the number of blocks for the 99-step double staircase, 98, 97, and all the staircases in sequence. To use this method for a 100-step problem means we would have to calculate all the prior constructions up to and including 99 steps. This would take a lot of calculations and even more patience. Look at the figure below and see if it helps you figure out a general rule that directly relates the staircase height to the number of blocks required for construction of the double staircase.

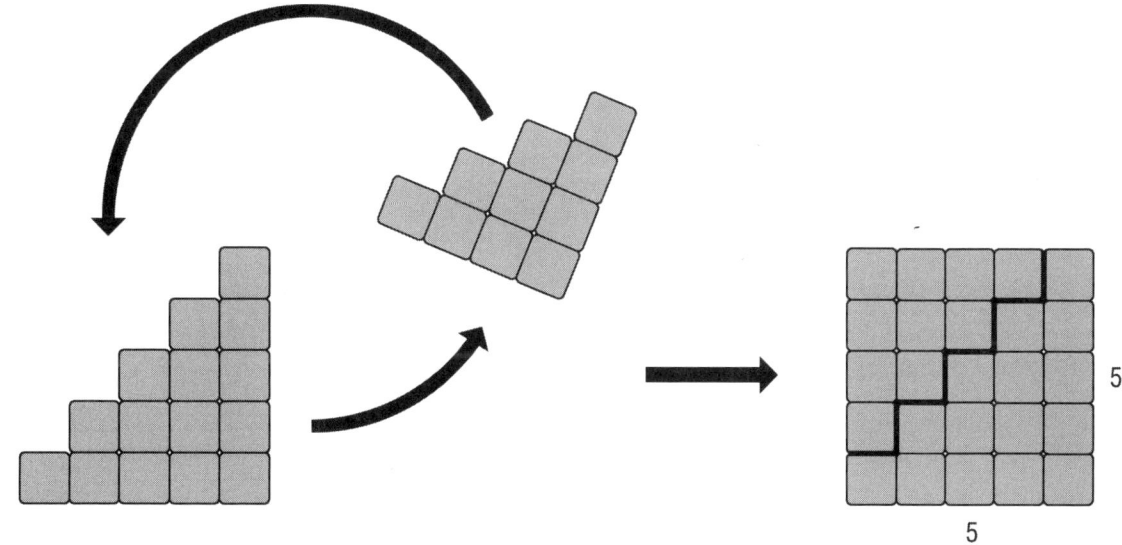

Problem Starter 44

Name:

Date:

FAVORITE PROBLEM

Describe a new problem that you created and share it with your class.

_____

_____

_____

_____

_____

_____

_____

_____

_____

_____

_____

_____